Praise for *T*

"As both an author and ghostwri̇̇ ̣   ̣ ̣   ̣ ̣ ̣ ̣ ̣ ̣ ̣ ̣ ̣ ̣ ̣ ̣ I can count. Julie Eason's *5 Author Freakouts* is like a secret ninja weapon. I'm signing a deal for my next manuscript right now, and this book will be sitting right on my desk to help me maintain my blood pressure from first word to last."

— Juju Hook, author of *Hot Flashes, Car Pools & Dirty Martinis*

"Speaking as an author who knows these 5 Freakouts as the old frenemies they are, I can vouch for every word—and not a one of them is fluff. Is this the most flat-out entertaining book I've read in a while? Yep. 'Fine, but will reading it actually make me a better writer?' Hell, yeah. There's gold in these pages."

— John David Mann, coauthor of the million-selling classic *The Go-Giver*

"Mindset and success coaching for writers all wrapped up in a powerful little book that will make you feel like you're not alone! Whether you write fiction or nonfiction, if it's your first book or your fifth, taming your freakouts will allow you to finish your work and get into the right mental state to share it with the world! Thanks, Julie!"

— Halle Eavelyn, transformational wealth coach and

author of *Red Goddess Rising* and *NutriGlamorous*

"Finally, someone's put a name to the emotional rollercoaster writers experience when writing and publishing a book. It's comforting to know that the freakouts are predictable, and we can handle them once we are aware of them. If you've ever stared at your book and wondered What the heck am I doing?! This book is for you."

— Terri Cole, Psychotherapist and author of *Boundary Boss: The Essential Guide to Talk True, Be Seen, and (Finally) Live Free*

"Knowing the factors that stop you in your tracks is probably more important than sitting down to write. In *The 5 Author Freakouts*, Julie Anne Eason correctly identifies what must just seem like recurring freak outs, no matter whether you're just starting out, or have written a dozen books. "Know your enemy" is the theme of this book, and Julie Anne effectively shows you where you're likely to get derailed and then effectively find your way out of the mess. You'll spin your wheels a lot less, because this book will not only give you direction, but inspiration that every writer goes through a similar sort of chaos. And that every writer should—and can—get out of that trap, if prepared. Read it, and be ready."

— Sean D'Souza, founder of Psychotactics.
com and author of *The Brain Audit*

"I would have taken another ten years to finish my book if it weren't for Julie. Her framework in this guide makes it so clear why so many of us miss the mark and never publish our dreams. Every person who ever thought of publishing a book, should read this. It's a framework that's been proven over decades of Julie's experience working with the most successful authors in every category. READ THIS NOW!"

— Amanda Holmes, CEO Chet Holmes, Int'l. And coauthor of *The Ultimate Sales Machine, 2nd ed.*

"Julie's book is a fun, quick read that gives you tools you need to get past the roadblocks that stop so many writers. Like a chat with a close friend, her book provides peace in knowing it's normal while helping you overcome your fears."

— April Shprintz, Author of *Magic Blue Rocks - The Secret to
Doing Anything* and Creator of the Generosity Culture®

"This book gives you the most important thing that every author needs. It's not a new technique, new vocabulary, sentence structure—it's not even a new platform.

It's belief.

Belief that your words are important—even vital. It's belief that you can do this. *The 5 Author Freakouts* reveals those 5 things that hold us back. Once we can see them, we can overcome them. Once you believe in yourself, you can get on with the important work of putting words on the page."

— Annie Grace, Author of *This Naked Mind* and *The Alcohol Experiment*

"*The 5 Author Freakouts* is a uniquely transformational book that turns struggling, frustrated, and sporadic writers into consistent, confident, and prolific authors. Julie showed me that I could do it with my books—after you read this book, you'll know you can too."

— Damian Boudreaux, Author of *The Magic List* and *Keep It Simple Selling*

THE 5 AUTHOR FREAKOUTS

Overcoming Procrastination, Self-Doubt,
And Imposter Syndrome On The Writer's Journey

Julie Anne Eason

www.ThanetHouseBooks.com
Thanet House Publishing

Paperback ISBN: 978-1-944602-16-1
Hardcover ISBN: 978-1-944602-59-8
Ebook ISBN: 978-1-944602-60-4
Audiobook ISBN: 978-1-944602-62-8

Cover Art by Francis Duvall & Laura Howard
Interior Layout by Laura Howard
Editing by Julie T. Willson

Publisher's Cataloging-In-Publication Data
(Prepared by The Donohue Group, Inc.)

Names: Eason, Julie Anne, author.
Title: The 5 author freakouts : how to overcome procrastination, self-doubt, and imposter syndrome on the writer's journey / Julie Anne Eason.
Other Titles: Five author freakouts
Description: [Garner, North Carolina] : Thanet House Publishing, [2022]
Identifiers: ISBN 9781944602161 (paperback) | ISBN 9781944602598 (hardcover) | ISBN 9781944602604 (ebook)
Subjects: LCSH: Authorship--Psychological aspects. | Procrastination. | Self-doubt. | Impostor phenomenon.
Classification: LCC PN171.P83 E37 2022 (print) | LCC PN171.P83 (ebook) | DDC 808.02019--dc23

For Me

This is the book I wish I could have read 30 years ago.

For You

When you are unsure, may this book be a reminder.

We got this!

CONTENTS

DEAR READER

Writing a book? Wrote a book? Thinking about it?

Congratulations!

You're my hero. More importantly, you're your readers' hero. Without you, they'll never get to read your book. (And what a shame that would be.)

Heroes come in all shapes and sizes, and in the case of authors, all genres. Fiction and nonfiction, romance and young adult, business and crafts— no matter what you're writing, it's going to be an adventure.

Like every hero, you're embarking on a quest. It's going to take courage, tenacity, and pigheaded determination to get it done. Even if you've published books before, each manuscript is a new journey.

It's a jungle out there. The quest will be full of danger and obstacles, but also excitement. And if you do make it through the challenges, you won't be the same person at the end of the journey.

You'll be a hero transformed.

You will have become the author your book needs you to be.

Like in every great adventure, the odds are stacked against you. What fun would it be otherwise?

There's a statistic floating around that says 97% of writers never finish their books. In my 30 years' experience as an author, ghostwriter, publisher, and coach, I've found that number is pretty close to the truth.

In spite of those odds, I know you're up to the challenge. Even in the dark nights of your soul when you want nothing more than to just give up, you won't. Because I'm going to arm you with tools and strategies to help you through any obstacle you come up against.

There are five challenges every successful author must overcome. They are the source of all writerly pain from indecision and self-doubt to procrastination and imposter syndrome. I call them the 5 Author Freakouts.

They will block you. They will mock you. They will make you question your sanity. But when you learn to recognize them and face them head-on, you'll win.

I've seen them over and over again with my clients. And I've been through them myself. In fact, I'm working through them even now as I write this book!

The freakouts are predictable: they happen precisely on time. Yet they look different from author to author. Sometimes the feeling is intense and other times merely annoying. They may have you flailing your arms, screaming at the computer screen, whining on social media, and metaphorically (I hope) tearing your hair out. Or your freakouts might be quiet, gently whispering less-than-helpful suggestions in your ear, pushing you into an endless editing loop.

They might even feel a little virtuous—they'll convince you that perfectionism is something to be proud of. You're not really procrastinating, it's just that you *care* so much about your book.

Freakouts are gremlins. Depending on how and what you feed them, they can be cute and cuddly or deadly. You can imagine they are fierce monsters trapping you and keeping you stuck. Or you can see them as minor challenges that help you grow into the author you need to be to support that book out in the world. Most of the time, they are a little of both.

Here's a secret—when you learn to recognize them and know how to communicate with them, you can make them work for you. They are eager to help, but will wreak havoc if you let them run free in your mind.

Here's another secret—all freakouts carry a gift. A secret surprise that is only revealed when you tame the freakout and escape its trap. But you can't escape the trap until you know you're in one.

And that's what this book will help you do. You're going to discover how to recognize all five author freakouts. By the end, you'll know when and why they happen. And you'll have tools to help you escape their clutches and receive the gifts they have for you.

Just so you know I'm in this with you, here's a little about me. I've been writing professionally since 1991. I've been a journalist, a magazine editor, a sales copywriter, and a ghostwriter. I also write my own nonfiction books. And I founded a company that ghostwrites and publishes nonfiction books for some of the most incredible leaders on the planet. They are who I have to thank for my discovery of the freakouts.

I started writing this book to help our clients understand the journey they're on. Because the more authors I worked with, the more clear the patterns became. They ALL experienced the same five obstacles with every book.

Even if I'd coached them through the journey before.

Even when they had the most amazing ghostwriter, they *still* succumbed to each freakout right on schedule.

After some informal research, I discovered that these freakouts happen to all writers. Nonfiction or fiction, screenwriters or content writers—it doesn't matter. If you're putting your voice out into the world, or you're helping clients put their messages into words, you're going to encounter these freakouts eventually. They always show up. All that matters is how fast you recognize them and whether or not you know how to tame them.

Every author I work with *insists* that they are above freaking out. They believe they're immune, too evolved to fall prey to something so silly. Yet when they look back at their journey, every one of them admits that yes, they did freak out a bit.

In fact, these freakouts happen in pretty much all creative projects. I find them everywhere, whether I'm writing or sewing or knitting or metalworking. But they show up in the worst way when I'm writing.

I think that's because I'm primarily a writer. It's what I do for a living. It's my identity. I hate that they still show up for me. But I know how to wrangle them. And soon you will too.

HOW DO YOU DEFEAT THE FREAKOUTS?

You defeat the freakouts through awareness and action. You have to know when you're experiencing one and how to handle it. When you can do those two things, the big scary monster turns into a cute, cuddly companion with a special gift for you. (Or at least a less scary sidekick.)

Look, being a writer is just ridiculously uncomfortable. If you're not that way in the beginning, you'll get there eventually. You're constantly reinventing yourself. Creating something out of nothing and having the audacity to sell it. Exposing yourself to strangers and declaring that something you thought of is worthy of being a book. Convincing yourself that your thoughts are worth writing down for posterity. Proving that your ideas can help other people.

Why would anyone do this to themselves voluntarily? We're writers. We can't help ourselves.

Even though we have to do battle with the freakouts alone, we writers are all in this together.

The world needs your words. We need your voice and your stories. Nothing in this world is more powerful than an idea authentically expressed.

That's what this book is for: to help you recognize the freakouts in the wild, and to give you powerful tools to overcome their tricksy ways so you can move forward with your work.

After you meet the freakouts, I'll give you some tools you can use whenever you'd like to find clarity, to gain confidence, to get what you need to keep going. These tools are interchangeable. Use the ones that speak to you the most in the moment.

WHO IS THIS BOOK FOR?

It's for anyone who struggles to start or finish their books.

It's for everyone who wonders whether their writing is any good.

It's for those of us with secret dreams we hope will come true.

And it's for anyone who's got something to say.

It's for all of us.

We band of brothers and sisters.

And it's for all of our readers.

Because they're out there. And they can't wait to read our books!

What I'm trying to say is that if you're not sure about this writing thing, it's okay. If you feel like you have no idea what you're doing, that's normal. If you'd rather wash the dishes than sit down and write for 10 minutes…yeah, I get it. Welcome to the club. You're in great company!

It doesn't matter if you're writing your first book or your tenth. It's always the same. The insecurities, the doubts, the little whispers in the back of your mind…

Am I doing it right?

What if someone finds out I have no idea what I'm doing?

What if people laugh at me? Am I just wasting my time?

These are your freakouts. They love to torture you, but only because they love you. They're doing their best to look out for you. And they will stop at nothing to keep you from finishing your book.

Let's fix that, shall we?

HOW THE FREAKOUTS WORK

Imagine you're getting ready to take an epic road trip. The car is all gassed up. You've got plenty of snacks. The tunes are cranked all the way up to 11. You slowly lower your shades over your eyes with an ever-so-cool smile. You put your foot on the gas.

Aaaaand…nothing. Pedal to the metal…still nothing. The wheels are spinning, but you're not moving forward. What gives?

This is how the freakouts operate. They quietly keep the brakes on your progress, even while you're doing everything you're supposed to do. They use a variety of tools and strategies to keep you spinning your wheels when you should be getting closer and closer to your destination.

It doesn't even matter if you're using a ghostwriter. I've had clients whose freakouts were so strong that even after paying me tens of thousands of dollars and spending years working on their book, they still abandoned the project! It baffles me.

But that's how strong your subconscious is. Your subconscious mind has its favorite ways of staying stuck, patterns that repeat over and over in your life, and the freakouts know exactly how to exploit them. Because the freakouts ARE your subconscious mind. You create them yourself. Which is kind of twisted, if you think about it.

Here you are trying to write. You *want* to finish this book. You *desire* to be a published author. If you already are a published author, you desire to be a prolific and beloved one. You want the fans, fame, and financial rewards. So what gives? Why are you creating roadblocks and resistance?

Because deep down, you *actually desire* something else that overrides your conscious desire. It's like you have one foot on the gas and one foot on the brake, and you wonder why you're spinning your wheels.

"What are you talking about?" you say. "That's ridiculous, Julie! I've been working on this idea for years. I absolutely WANT to write it. I want it published."

Do you? Do you really? Because if you're stuck or facing resistance, it's entirely possible that somewhere deep down inside you, something else is overriding that desire. And the freakouts are going to exploit it all the way through the process. They're going to mock you and whisper horrible things into your brain like…

What are you thinking?

You're no writer.

No one's going to read this garbage.

Screw that! If you can uncover what's going on, it will be easier to stare those guys down and get on with your work.

You want to finish this project you've been working on, yes? You really want it?

Okay, great. You've got one foot solidly on the gas pedal. So ask yourself these two questions to find the foot that's on the brake. Actually *do* this exercise. It will change everything.

WHAT'S THE DOWNSIDE OF FINISHING?

If I finish my book...

...I'll have to find a publisher—and I don't know how.

...I'll have to show it to people—and they might laugh at me.

...people might expect another book—and I don't know if I have another one in me.

...I'll prove my father wrong, show him that I actually AM a writer—and I don't want to lose his approval.

...I might be tempted to quit my job to write full-time—and what if I starve?

What else?

WRITE YOUR ANSWERS HERE

WHAT'S THE PAYOFF IF YOU NEVER COMPLETE THE BOOK?

If I don't finish the book...

...I don't have to endure the humiliation of finding a publisher, which means I don't ever have to face rejection.

...I get to keep my words to myself—and I love my words!

...no one will be able to judge me, which means I'm always going to be a brilliant writer, even if it's only in my mind.

...I get to stay in my stable, secure day job—and that means I'll stay safe and be able to feed myself.

What else?

WRITE YOUR ANSWERS HERE

Take your time. There are probably lots of payoffs for you staying stuck, and they may elude you for a while. You might easily uncover a few, but then there's one big sticky payoff that's really good at hiding. And that's the one controlling the show. It's okay if you don't uncover everything right away. If you're not used to this kind of introspection, it can feel strange, and you might not know what actually counts as a payoff.

Here's a hint: The payoff is an attitude or belief that was planted in your brain when you were a child and is somehow related to your physical survival.

For example, payoffs often revolve around what other people will think of us. Why? Because if people don't approve of us, we may be rejected and thrown out of the tribe. And way back in caveman days, that meant certain death. The tribe (whether that's a family or a community) represents safety and security.

So deep down, who are you afraid might reject you? An agent? A publisher? Your parents? Your children? Your partner? Your friends? Look there first.

Another place the payoffs hide is in our sense of physical security. If you're dreaming of becoming a famous novelist, but your entire childhood you were told, "Writers don't make money. Your Uncle Arthur was a writer, and he died a penniless drunk. You don't want to be like him!" well of course your subconscious is going to try and keep you from following in that poor sod's footsteps.

If Mom wants you to be a doctor and you want to be a writer, who's going to win out?

The answer is different for everyone, because it depends a lot on how you grew up and what your relationship with your mom was. But chances are pretty good that Mom is going to win. You'll become a doctor, or at least try to. Just to win her love or keep her approval. And you'll probably justify it by saying, "She's right—I need a solid career."

Take the time to explore why your "deep down" might be trying to sabotage your best efforts. Because you probably already have all the time management, productivity, writing, and marketing advice you need to be mega-successful. And it's all probably good advice, IF you have both feet on the gas. But if you have one foot on the brake, you're not going anywhere.

The secret to breaking free and loving your creative pursuits is an inside job. (Why they don't teach this stuff in school, I'll never know.)

I'll be sharing lots more tools you can use to outsmart the freakouts throughout the rest of this book. But if you start here and *actually do the exercise above* (ahem, I know you want to skip it and do it later), everything else will seem simple and work beautifully. If you don't uncover the source of your resistance, then nothing in this book (or any other) will help much. Because no book, workshop, course, or seminar will ever be stronger than your own subconscious mind.

This subconscious sabotage doesn't just happen with writing, by the way. It's a phenomenon that continually repeats itself in our lives until we uncover what the hell is going on and put a stop to it. There's nothing wrong with you. It's just part of being human.

You want to attract your dream partner, but you keep ending up with codependent assholes.

You want to lose weight but can't kick your junk food habit.

You want more money but can't seem to find a better job.

It's all the same. If you want something and you've tried to get it but it's not happening, look underneath. Where is your subconscious foot on the brake? How are you putting up blocks and resistance? What's the payoff for NOT getting what you want?

Okay, let's get back to writing. Because these freakouts are real, even though your mind is creating them. And here's the cool thing—once you learn how to recognize and move past them, not only will your writing progress but everything else in your life will too.

THE FREAKOUT TACTICS

Here's how the freakouts show up. You may have experienced one or all of them already. Some might be waiting to ambush you later on in the process. See if you recognize any of these.

CONFUSION OR LACK OF CLARITY

Freakout #1 is all about this strategy. Lack of clarity will keep you spinning and reaching for your favorite distractions, especially early in the first draft process. It's incredibly common to have too many ideas, too many characters, too many plotlines. And if you fall in love with all of them, you won't be able to make critical decisions.

You're on a hamster wheel. It seems like you're making progress, but in fact you're just spinning in place. And once you beat it, don't think it can't come back. You can spin out into confusion at any point, so you're going to need some tools to get you back on track. Don't worry, I've got you covered.

OVERWHELM

We're all so damn busy all the time that most of us practically live in overwhelm. (I pledge allegiance to the flag of the United State Of Overwhelm!) If that hits a little too close to home, realize that the freakouts are going to use this to their advantage.

Whether you're overwhelmed with work, family, politics, or anything else—it all builds up, and it's a tough cycle to break. If you're really committed to an overwhelm lifestyle, your physical health will start to decline, and eventually your body will force you to take a break (hopefully not in the form of a heart attack or other life-threatening issue.) But make no mistake—you will be forced to let some things slide.

The freakouts know this. So your book will often be the very first thing to get put on the back burner "just until things calm down." That might be fine. Or it might not. It all depends on your priorities and what that book represents. Is it a hobby? Or is it how you feed yourself and your family?

I've had clients who put their revisions off for years because of one circumstance after another.

I'll do it as soon as…

…this product launch is over.

…the kids get out of school.

…the kids get back in school.

…I go on vacation.

…I get back from vacation.

…I get my boob job (seriously).

Some of them finally did finish their books; others have not (yet).

The more important the book is—the tighter your deadline—the more fiercely you need to guard your time. When something's gotta give, make sure it's not your book.

DISTRACTION

How does your mind deal with overwhelm? Distraction. That's also how it deals with fear and boredom and overwhelming emotions and just about everything else.

Your mind is tricky: it knows your favorite distractions. They might be mindless like checking social media, playing games on your phone, binging your favorite TV show, or partying with friends. You might also get stuck in priority-shifting distractions like family or business matters. There's nothing like preschool children or a product launch at work to keep your mind otherwise engaged.

Even your daily workout can be a distraction, depending on how you're using it. Is that workout a time for you to fuel your body and mind for the day ahead? Is it a time to unload after a stressful day? Or do you tell yourself, "I can't write today because, you know, I have to hit the gym," as if it's a task that will take all day (which it totally can if you're procrastinating that as well as your book).

The freakouts will use any distraction they can to pull you off course, but it's not like that's hard work for them. You provide them with plenty of opportunities.

I picture them sitting back, chilling with Netflix and a vat of mint chip ice cream, just waiting for me to get serious about a project. Then when it looks like I'm about to make some real progress, all they have to do is pause their show and whisper, "Yeah, but what about that client?" Or "Have you checked the comments on that last social post?" And my day could be completely thrown off.

I might get back to my project…or I might not. Unless I'm putting my own writing first, before clients or students, it will be a toss-up whether I get to it or not.

BURNOUT

Like distraction, burnout can happen from an overly stressful life or from the act of writing itself. Either way, guess what's getting dropped first? Your book.

It can be a serious condition where you really do need to step away and center yourself. Give yourself time to recover before you wind up with worse problems than just not writing. The secret to beating burnout is to stop it before it even gets to the overwhelm stage. And that requires strong self-awareness.

The freakouts love burnout, because you do all the work for them. And once you do sorta get your act together, all they have to do is whisper the word "burnout" to make you wonder whether you're pushing yourself too hard. Once you've recovered, you'll never want to get back to that point again.

So every time you can't think of what to write next will be an opportunity to wonder, *Am I burning out?*

SELF-DOUBT

Ah, self-doubt—a writer's constant companion.

Who am I to write a book?

My plot is so lame.

There are so many people who are much more experienced than me.

There are already so many books on this topic.

I must be crazy to think I can do this.

I'm never going to finish.

I'm a hack. A loser.

Whatever.

Self-doubt is just a part of life as a creative person. You can let it take over your life, or you can recognize it for what it is—just a bunch of noise in your head.

The freakouts are going to use this against you. Be ready. No matter how self-confident you are, at some point you'll doubt yourself. It's up to you whether you let it control you or not.

John Steinbeck once wrote, "I am not a writer. I've been fooling myself and other people." He also said, "I am assailed by my own ignorance and inability." Yeah, that inability won him a Pulitzer Prize.

IMPOSTER SYNDROME

What if people find out I don't know what I'm doing?

I need more practice, more experience.

What if someone in the media asks a question I don't know the answer to?

What if I make some horrible mistake and embarrass myself in front of the whole world?

I get it—you don't know everything there is to know about your subject. But that doesn't mean you can't write about it. There will *always* be people ahead of you. And there will always be people behind you.

Who can you help? That's the question.

One of my mentors, Sean D'Souza, taught me that imposter syndrome is just being aware of the gap between what you know and what you don't know. And if you're a reasonably humble person, you're going to perceive a pretty big gap.

Maya Angelou once confessed:

"I have written eleven books, but each time I think, *Uh-oh, they're going to find out now. I've run a game on everybody and they're going to find me out.*"

Yeah, lady, that Presidential Medal of Freedom looks pretty sketchy. You sure you can write? Confidence is gained in hindsight.

What most of us don't do is really *own* our expertise. We don't give ourselves enough credit for what we do know, what we have gone through, and how we can help people. We don't give ourselves enough credit for our imaginations and stick-to-itiveness.

We don't recognize how far we've come. So the freakouts have an easy job of showing us the gap and making us feel unworthy of writing that book. Don't let them.

PROCRASTINATION

Procrastination is the great-granddaddy of all the freakouts' tactics! Everything leads to it. But before you can stop it, you have to be aware that it's happening. What's your procrasti-distraction of choice?

Procrasti-scrolling?

How about procrasti-cleaning? (My house is never so neat and tidy as when I'm on a deadline.)

There's procrasti-eating, procrasti-drinking, procrasti-research, procrasti-worldbuilding, procrasti-parenting.

The list goes on and on. Eating, drinking, research, and parenting are not bad things. We have to do them. It's the intention behind the action that makes it either legit or procrastination. Be honest with yourself.

Yeah, I'd really love to watch this Disney flick for the twenty-seventh time…but I should probably be writing right now instead.

MICROMANAGING AND OVERCONTROLLING

Some writers feel like they have to control every little piece of the project, including the editing and the publishing. They nitpick a third-tier minor character's eye color. They rigidly stick to their outline, even when it's clearly not working. They second-guess and question every comment from beta readers or editors.

Freakout #4 loves this technique because even if you manage to finish your draft, the book will have to fight its way through production. It all boils down to lack of trust—in your intuition, your editor, or your publishing team. Don't make their lives miserable just because of a freakout. Trust them to do their jobs. Your book will be better for it.

IGNORING MARKETING

Even if you write the most brilliant book of all time, if no one is there to read it, then it's doomed to failure. Marketing blindness is a special tool of Freakout #5, but it settles in earlier. This strategy subconsciously sabotages your book's success once it's finally done.

If you haven't started building a following for the book you're writing, start now. It takes time, and you want to be well underway by the time your draft is finished.

The only excuse for not marketing and building a following for you and your books is because you don't know you're supposed to be doing it.

Guess what? As of the moment you read that last sentence, you no longer have that excuse. (Sorry, not sorry.)

RUSHING THROUGH THE PROJECT

The payoff for rushing is that you don't have to take responsibility for the quality. This mindset is encouraged by meme-culture language like "hustle harder" and "take imperfect action" and "just ship it." There's wisdom in those sayings…to a point. But it's easy to fall into the trap of outrunning yourself.

The digital world is impermanent. It's here today and gone tomorrow.

Make a mistake? Delete the post.

Need to revise your e-book? Unpublish it, fix it, and resubmit.

We live in a world of easy iteration, and we've become accustomed to the blinding speed of change. But writing a book takes time. And you're not doing yourself any favors rushing through it.

Books are permanent: once they're in print and out in the world, you can't pull them back. And that is terrifying to people accustomed to living with impermanence.

My friends know I will be the first to say, "That's good enough. Move on!" But that attitude needs to be balanced with care and nurturing. Not everything should be rushed. Sometimes you need to take the time to improve your book so you can produce something you're proud of. I'm not talking about perfectionism—there's no such thing as perfect. I'm talking about high quality blended with a dash of good enough.

At the root of all these freakout tactics is straight-up fear.

What if I'm making a huge mistake?

What if no one reads it?

What if I make a wrong decision?

What if I'm just embarrassing myself?

What will people think?

What if everyone loves it and they want ANOTHER book?

What if I can't deliver on those expectations?

WHAT IF IT'S NOT SAFE?

Blah blah blah…

Fear is a healthy self-protection mechanism. Fear keeps us from touching hot stoves, running out into traffic, and eating that two-week-old pizza in the fridge that's "probably still good." And it keeps us from making bad decisions that could affect our future, *based on what happened in the past.*

One of my favorite authors, Kyle Cease, likes to say, "Your mind can measure what you might lose, but it can't measure what you could gain."

In other words, sure your fear might be right, and publishing this book might send you into a spiral of bad decisions that end in ruin. You've seen it happen before. Uncle Arthur was not a pretty picture.

But you are not him. And what if publishing this book is the best thing that ever happens to you? What if it starts you on a path to fame and fortune? What if you're destined to change the world with your words?

You can't measure or predict just how amazing your future could be, because you only have your past experiences to draw from. You are not Uncle Arthur. Last time is not this time. The past does not dictate the future, unless you allow it to. If you do, the freakouts win.

If all these freakout tactics are freaking you out, don't worry. I'm going to give you lots of strategies you can use to defeat them throughout this book, starting with the very best one right now. Keep reading!

YOUR MAGIC LIST

Let me ask you a question (or five).

Do you want to be more prolific?

Do you want to write faster?

Do you want to make more money?

Would you like to have a better relationship with your family?

Do you want a happy, healthy, abundant life?

You do? Sweet! Because I'm about to share with you the fastest way to break through the bullshit and have the most amazing life ever.

Take off your shoes and put them on the wrong feet.

Really. Like, do it right now.

I know what you're thinking, but do it anyway.

(Please, I'm begging. This could be the most life-changing thing you ever do. So take your damn shoes off and put them on the wrong feet!)

Good! Now, how does that look? Wrong? Bad? Stupid?

Stand up and walk around a bit. (For real, just do it.)

How does it feel? Terrible? Uncomfortable? Out of balance?

What if they were a great-looking, really expensive pair of shoes and you put them on the wrong feet? Would they still look bad? Would it still feel off?

Of course it would! Want to know why?

Because it's not what's on the outside that matters; it's what's on the…

…INSIDE!

The inside matters most.

Okay, now put those guys back on the right feet. How do they look now? How do they feel?

Better! Correct! Comfortable!

Here's the thing—most people wake up and put their lives on the wrong feet every single day. They put their families on the wrong feet, and that's why they fight all the time. They put their job on the wrong feet, and that's why they're not thriving.

You do it too. I know you do, because I do it. Everybody does it. It's part of human nature. And when life is on the wrong feet, it doesn't feel right. It feels unnatural. It feels *off* somehow. We all dress up on the outside but leave the most important parts of us—the inside—to chance. We don't think we have control over what's going on inside, but we do!

When life is on the right feet, everything flows. Life is wonderful! Deals come together. People get along. Relationships improve.

And when your writing is on the right feet, the words come easy. The plot unwinds naturally. You can write a terrifying villain, soft-hearted heroine, or quirky sidekick anytime you want. You can shift from one scene to the next, one framework to the next, easily.

Sounds pretty great, huh?

I know you probably think I'm dreaming or that I don't live in the real world. But listen, I've been writing words professionally for most of my life now. I've done it the hard way. I've gritted my teeth and forced my way through. I've worked for years with my writing on the wrong feet. And I've also done it the easy way. I've experienced flow and grace and ease. And let me tell you, that way is SO much better!

You don't have to be some kind of writing superhero to experience this for yourself. And it doesn't have to happen by chance. You can control it. You can put your writing on the right feet in a matter of *seconds* once you know how. And I'm about to teach you how right now.

But first, I have to give credit to the guy who taught me this. His name is Damian Boudreaux, and he uses the "shoes on the wrong feet" metaphor to teach car salespeople how to sell more cars. He uses it to help terminally ill people face their fears and live their lives to the fullest. And he uses it to help rid entire school systems of bullying and low achievement.

Say hello, Damian!

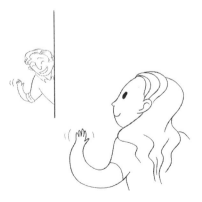

He and I write books together, and I'm forever grateful that he shared his philosophy with me. It has changed everything in my life and my career. What you're about to learn is his gift to the world, not mine. But he has given me permission to share it far and wide—because *everyone* should know how to live life to the fullest with no stress, anger, or fear.

This method is pretty much a magic wand that you can use *anywhere* and *anytime* you want to change what's happening around you.

It's the master key to releasing fear, overwhelm, procrastination, imposter syndrome, and self-doubt.

It's the key to overcoming fears around marketing and sales.

It's the key to dealing with your in-laws and creating more harmony in your home.

It's even the key to handling stressful situations you can't control like politics, taxes, and social media.

It's your master key to life.

Ready to learn it?

The first step is to write down 60 positive characteristics describing *who you are at your best*. Use only adjectives. (You're a writer—this will be a piece of cake. Usually we have to start out by describing what an adjective is.) The adjective part is important because you're describing who you ARE, not what you do.

So you can say, "I am witty" or "I am insightful." But not "I am a writer" (noun) or "I am writing" (verb).

You can do it right here in the book or find a piece of paper and a pen. You could even type it into your phone. It doesn't really matter as long as you can get access to your list whenever you want it. Just do it right now. Don't put it off. This is going to change your life.

This is your Magic List. It's your identity. It's who you truly are at your core. It's the foundation of your whole BEING. And it's key to putting your writing and your life on the right feet.

Here's what a bit of my list looks like.

Who I Am At My Best

I am smart. I am funny. I am lighthearted. I am creative. I am prolific. I am giving. I am beautiful. I am intuitive. I am magical. I am loving. I am kind. I am adventurous.

You get the idea. Just keep writing until you get to 60 descriptors. Take as much time as you need.

And remember, this is who you are *at your best*. It's okay if you don't feel that way all the time. It's okay if you don't feel that way now. Just use your beautiful imagination and write what comes naturally to mind.

Scan me for a printable Magic List.

I AM _____ I AM _____ I AM _____

I AM _____ I AM _____ I AM _____

I AM _____ I AM _____ I AM _____

I AM _____ I AM _____ I AM _____

I AM _____ I AM _____ I AM _____

I AM _____ I AM _____ I AM _____

I AM _____ I AM _____ I AM _____

I AM _____ I AM _____ I AM _____

I AM _____ I AM _____ I AM _____

I AM _____ I AM _____ I AM _____

I AM _____ I AM _____ I AM _____

I AM _____ I AM _____ I AM _____

I AM _____ I AM _____ I AM _____

I AM _____ I AM _____ I AM _____

I AM _____ I AM _____ I AM _____

I AM _____ I AM _____ I AM _____

I AM _____ I AM _____ I AM _____

I AM _____ I AM _____ I AM _____

I AM _____ I AM _____ I AM _____

I AM _____ I AM _____ I AM _____

Did you get to 60? Most people start to struggle after about 20. Writers tend to shift into synonyms…at least I do. And that's okay. You can build your list over time. Whenever you come across a new adjective that fits, you can add it to your list. Mine is over 100 words now. Damian's is over 200.

Great—you've got your list, or at least a solid start. Now what? Read over your words. In fact, read them out loud.

Who is the person you're describing? What can *that* person achieve? Is it possible for *that* person to make more money? Have better relationships? Accomplish their goals? Dream bigger? Be happier? Can *that* person show up more confident, helpful, energetic, focused? Can that person write a best seller?

Who is that person?

It's YOU!

Really own that. Take a moment and bask in the glorious feeling that you are an amazing human being.

So how does this list help you do your job day to day, moment by moment? How does it help you write faster, better, and without struggle? It simply reminds you of who you are already.

There's the version of you in this moment and maybe that version is struggling a little bit. And there's the *best* version of you as represented on your list. Deep down inside, you ARE all those things. When you align yourself with the words on your list, you can't help but flow with the natural current of life. The words come easier. You stay focused longer. And inspired ideas just pop up out of the blue.

Of course, we're all humans, so we don't always stay in alignment with our best selves. Sometimes we wake up grumpy. A pile of bills makes us feel like we don't make enough money. Maybe that means we're not good enough. Maybe we should get a night-shift job instead of writing. Sometimes things happen that make us sad. Or we get distracted from our writing by social media. Or we just feel uninspired and wonder if we'll ever have another good idea in our entire lives.

It's totally normal to slip into those not-ideal states. We all forget who we are from time to time. We do it dozens, if not hundreds, of times a day. Our lives slip off track and we just have to stop, refocus, and start again.

You want to pull yourself back into alignment with your best self so life can flow. The good news is the more you practice it, the faster you'll get at realigning. Until one day you find that you're being your best self most of the time.

I'm not talking about ignoring the fact that your beloved pet passed away or blowing off the bills that are due. You can still acknowledge those things *and* be your best self. Dealing with sadness or anxiety will be much easier when you're in that best-self state.

So how do you do it? How do you actually *use* your list?

First off, anytime you're feeling out of sorts—you yell at your family or you're angry, frustrated, bored, listless, anxious, or hopeless—stop and think, *This is not me. This is not who I am at my best.*

Then pull out your list and start reading the words out loud. Breathe deeply and read slowly enough for the words to really sink in.

I am smart. I am kind. I am funny. I am creative. I am productive. I am alert. I am energetic. I am inspired…

Remind yourself that this is who you truly are.

After about the fifth word, you'll feel yourself starting to relax. Usually after the tenth word or so, you're back in alignment and feeling pretty good. You might even wonder why you were so out of sorts at all. That's how you remember who you truly are. That's how you realign and put your shoes on the right feet.

BE/DO/HAVE

Those three little words are the secret to change. They're the secret to getting anything you want, really.

But our conscious minds, our egos, want it the other way around. They want to Have/Do/Be. We want to HAVE proof that we're a best-selling writer…then we'll DO the work to BE one. We want proof that what we're doing is going to work out before we put in the effort.

But creativity doesn't work that way.

There's a whole industry full of marketers who have figured out how to hack their way onto best-seller lists—from Amazon to *New York Times*. All you have to do is pay them enough money and your book is guaranteed to make the list—whether it's any good or not. This is a prime example of Have/Do/Be. If you're guaranteed a best seller, you'll *do* the work to get it out as quickly as possible so you can *be* that.

But guess what? Having the title "best-selling author" after your name doesn't actually mean you've sold a lot of books, that your book is popular, or that people love it and are recommending it to their friends. It doesn't mean you're *actually* changing lives. Best-seller status has become a vanity metric based on manipulation and carefully curated lists. Focus on Be/Do/Have and you'll go a lot further in your career and life.

So what does Be/Do/Have actually mean? If you want your book to be popular and sell lots of copies, you first need to BE the author who has achieved that. In other words…

> BE who you are at your best.
>
> BE the person on your list.
>
> BE in alignment with your best self.

Mentally picture it. Emotionally feel how awesome it is to receive fan mail and to speak on stages in front of thousands. First imagine it visually, then feel it emotionally. Who do you need to BE to bust out another 3,000 words today? Who do you need to BE to finish writing that fight scene? Even without *having* proof that you can do it.

Once you have the emotional state anchored in your body, choose three words from your list that will help you achieve that state you've just imagined. Put them together and read them out loud like this:

I am *smart*, *creative*, and *focused*…so I can help my readers change their lives.

I am *devious*, *playful*, and *imaginative*…so I can make the reader fall in love with the villain.

I am *confident*, *excited*, and *organized*…so I can finish this draft today.

How does that feel? Does your body feel the way you imagined? Are you in alignment physically and emotionally? Yes? Then get to work—GO!

When you can BE in alignment and sustain that desired state over time, you'll naturally want to DO the things necessary to defeat the freakouts and create a work of art. The natural by-product of that is to HAVE the outcome you pictured and felt.

You are a human BEing, not a human DOing.

Stop thinking, *What do I have to DO today to finish this chapter?*

Instead think, *Who do I have to BE and what state do I need to BE IN to complete this chapter?*

Now that you have this incredible tool at your disposal, it's time to meet the freakouts. First, I'm going to introduce you to each one. Then I'll show you more of my favorite tools for dealing with them.

Ready? Let's go!

MEET THE FREAKOUTS

AUTHOR FREAKOUT #1
SQUINTY MAGOO

I will do ANYTHING to avoid writing this book. I will read and research. I will scroll through social media. I will do my laundry and clean out my car. I will finish client work before my own. I will care for my children and parents.

And I will scribble down a few notes now and then so I can lie to myself.

See? I'm making progress…it's just slow progress. All good things come to those who wait.

I just don't have time today.

You know, work is really crazy right now. As soon as this project is out the door…

…THEN I'll make this book my #1 priority.

…THEN I'll give it my undivided attention.

…THEN I'll have the bandwidth to finally focus and write every day.

What a load of crap!

I know how to do this book writing thing. I've written dozens of books for clients. It's WHAT I DO. And I know what this is—it's a ritual I recognize.

It's the birthplace of every book ever written...and the death of every book not written.

It's **Author Freakout #1: Squinty Magoo**. I call him Squinty for short. If you're not old enough to remember the old cartoon *Mr. Magoo*, he was this nearsighted old man who got himself into funny situations because he insisted on going through life without his glasses.

One of my clients calls this the "stumbling and fumbling" stage. You think you have your book outlined and you try to write, but it doesn't quite work. Then you try a different outline. Then you decide maybe you should be writing this *other book*. It can last for years, especially with first-time authors.

Poor Squinty can never find his glasses. He forever lacks clarity—until you help him find it.

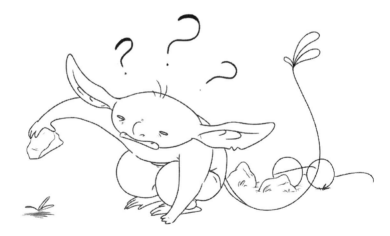

I'm intimately familiar with him because I help other authors through this obstacle all the time. People talk to me about what they do and who they help, and somehow I can instantly "download" their books in my mind in complete detail. I can visualize the structure and the flow. I can see how the chapters should lay out. I can picture the publishing and distribution model—all of it. But because they're still stuck in this freakout, they can't.

I do the same for my books too, of course. I know in my head and in my heart what each book is supposed to do. I know who it will help. I've outlined it to death. I've fantasized about the formatting and cover design.

But until I escape this freakout, until I help Squinty Magoo find clarity, I will continue to NOT WRITE.

In the beginning, there is infinite possibility. Your book can be *anything*.

It could be funny, it could be serious, it could be academic, it could be a comic book…

The only thing you know it can't be is *boring*!

And that's tough because what is "boring" anyway? How do you measure that? I mean, *you* think your idea is brilliant—but you also thought making grilled cheese in the toaster was brilliant too! (Trust me, it's not. True story.)

You've read boring books before. You probably had to read them in school. So you know what it looks like when you see it in the wild. You can even recognize it in other people's work. But it's difficult to do on your own, especially when nothing's been written yet. You're just in the idea stage.

So we float in the deep, dark sea of infinite possibilities. We dive deep into our experience, looking for magic. We stumble around in the dark, searching for the answer to Squinty's Big Question: *What should I write about?*

We know in general what we want to write. We want to share our stories.

We want to help people avoid the pain we suffered or enjoy the pleasures we've found.

We want to teach.

We want to entertain.

Most of all we want our self-expression to find an audience— an audience that *loves* it.

We desperately need clarity.

Squinty shows up in a few different disguises.

HE CAN SHOW UP AS TOO MANY IDEAS.

As I'm writing this, I have three books I want to write (and probably another three dozen I'm noodling over). All three have an audience. All three will help people. All three are based on my story. And I've known about them for over two years now. In two years, I could have written ALL of them. But instead I played the victim for Squinty and switched focus from one to the next to the next—back and forth and back again—agonizing over which one I should write first.

And I can think of at least four people I've spoken to this month who are doing exactly the same thing. They know they can write. They know they have lots of books in them. But they have too many ideas, so they procrastinate and don't do *any of them*. It's like they're frozen in place. They're freaking out.

SQUINTY CAN ALSO SHOW UP
AS A SEEMING LACK OF IDEAS.

Everyone says I should write a book, but what would I say?

What do I have to share that anyone would possibly find interesting or helpful?

Sound familiar?

Look, I've written books for all kinds of businesspeople. I've even written books for a locksmith! Everyone has something important to share. Deep down we know this. We know what we could write about. That's not the problem.

For nonfiction writers, the problem is we know too much about a given topic. We have so much experience with parenting or cooking or business or whatever that we completely forget what it's like to NOT KNOW.

We forget that even just one tiny inconsequential nugget of information from our brains can completely change someone else's life for the better. One tip about how you learned to quit drinking alcohol could heal a broken marriage. One healthy recipe could save someone from a heart attack.

And fiction writers do the same thing. They usually know WAY more about the characters and worlds than they really need to. Worldbuilding, historical research, character sketches... *Wait! I need to make a topographically correct map of the entire planet before I start writing!* (Yeah, busted.)

The thing about author freakouts is they're all in our heads. We make them up out of nothing. But they talk to us like they're real. They say things like, "Yeah yeah, but there are tips and recipes and information *everywhere*. The internet is bloated with information. Why should anyone care about what you have to say? You're just someone who figured out a hack for saving money. So what? People can read any number of blogs or books on the same idea. YOU'RE NOTHING SPECIAL."

Oh, but you are! Very special.

And the massive amount of information and entertainment available is precisely why we need you to write your book. Because people resonate with other people. Everything is energy, after all. And certain people are coded to resonate with you and no one but you.

There's no one like you anywhere in the world. So if YOU don't write your book, those people may never find the answers they seek.

How many times have you heard/read/thought that you should take better care of yourself? Probably dozens of times a week! And yet you completely ignore most of those messages. It's not until you come across that one special messenger—the one who resonates with you—that you are finally spurred to take action.

That book matters.

YOUR book matters!

And that is what gives Squinty the power to keep you spinning in your own head. Playing in the pool of infinite possibilities… forever.

The best way to escape this freakout and get on with writing your book is to get out of your head and into the heads of your readers. This is what I call outside-in thinking, and it works for both fiction and nonfiction.

Instead of "What should I write about?" you ask, "Who is my intended audience and what do they need to know?"

Taking the focus off yourself frees you from the tyranny of "doing it right" and "not being boring." Putting the focus on the reader gets you out of the sea of possibilities and gives you some boundaries to work with.

Think about it this way—a river can't flow without the hard boundaries of the banks and the riverbed. And your writing can't flow without knowing these things:

Nonfiction

- Who is your reader?
- What problem are they trying to solve?
- Can you help them solve it?
- What do they need to know first?

Fiction

- Who is the protagonist?
- What is their problem?
- How do they take the first step?

THAT'S what you should write. Your book is not about you; it's about the hero. And the book's hero is either your fictitious character or your reader.

You don't completely escape Squinty's clutches until you leave the outlining and planning stages behind you. Yes, you need to plan. Yes, you should outline. But it's easy to stay stuck in the planning phase for months or years.

So many books die prematurely because the author just keeps tweaking the outline. They *felt like* they were making progress. They *told themselves* that the delays were necessary because they cared about producing a quality book. But at some point, this is just perfectionism—and it's your enemy, not your friend.

At some point, you have to start writing.

The outline is a tool, nothing more. It's a map to get you from page one to The End as simply as possible. No one is ever going to see that outline. Planning can move you forward or hold you back. And that's what this freakout is all about. You choose when it's over.

Just when you think you've got the clarity you need, Squinty isn't quite done with you. There's a second part to this freakout.

I can teach anyone how to pull a brilliant book out of their head, but that's not what's *really* holding them back. The real issue is that whether you know it or not, you're about to embark on an incredible hero's journey of transformation. You will *not* be the same person by the time your book is published.

As with every hero's journey, you'll be tested and challenged. You'll climb to incredible heights and be rewarded with the most beautiful views. You'll also crawl through the lowest valleys, skinning your knees on the rocks and scratching your skin on the thorny underbrush. You might meet some terrifying beasties along the way or enjoy a pint of ale, and I'm sure you'll make some new friends.

But before any of that can happen, every hero has to *accept the call*. Bilbo had to step out his front door and willingly journey into the unknown. Harry Potter had to run headlong into a brick wall on Platform 9¾. The trauma therapist has to be willing to talk about her past abuse.

You have to accept the call and *decide* you're going to go on this adventure, no matter where it leads.

Just like Harry and Bilbo, you will have many adventures. You may write many books. But you have to start with the one in front of you at this moment. Say yes and commit to this one adventure—see it through—and then you can take on the next one when you're ready.

What does all that mean in practical terms?

> If you're switching back and forth between books like, "Should I write this one or that one…"

> If you're coming up with too many ideas that keep you stuck in the outlining or worldbuilding stage like, "Just a little more research and I'll be ready to start…"

> If you've been noodling and outlining for months or years…

> Or if you want to write a book but have no idea what to say or how to start…

Those are all signs that you haven't fully committed to the adventure. You haven't accepted the call yet. You're still deciding *if* you're going to write this book.

Once you decide (for real) that you're doing this (no matter what), the guides you need will appear. It's magical how you'll meet a book coach or see an ad for a writing course. Or your friend will share their experiences writing their most recent book. Or, you know, you just start writing.

I help people write their books all the time. But I can't help them if they're not committed.

And here's the thing—no one *has to* write a book. If this author thing is just something you want to dabble with, it's totally fine. And there's nothing wrong with deciding it's truly not the right time. Stop beating yourself up over it. Decide to refuse the call, and get on with your life.

But if you *do* have to write your book, because your soul won't rest until you do—if your book is burning to get out of you— then just say "yes" and get started. The beginning will probably suck, and that is okay. At least you'll be moving forward instead of fumbling and stumbling around in your head.

You will know you're past Freakout #1 when you've *committed* to your idea and outline…and you're actually writing.

Squinty's gift is clarity. Enjoy it. Use it. And keep it handy. You're going to need it regularly along the way.

So there you are, writing along as happy as can be. The words are flowing, the imagery and metaphors are inspiring. Everything is going great!

All of a sudden, you feel a tingling at the back of your neck. Your chest gets a little tight. Something's wrong… Welcome to Freakout #2.

AUTHOR FREAKOUT #2
SPEEDY MCRACERPANTS

About 10 years into writing my first book (the one that took 16 years), I noticed a behavior pattern. It revolved around the number three.

I would write three paragraphs, then almost ritualistically read over them and revise them for hours at a time. Sometimes days would go by before I was done revising those three paragraphs. Then when I reached three pages, I'd repeat the ritual—edit, revise, obsess, and *maybe* consider writing the next three paragraphs. That would go on for a while...until I finished the first three chapters.

Sounds great. I'm into the story. I'm making progress. It won't be long till that draft is done, right? Nope. That's when I would put the whole project away for one reason or another.

I graduated high school. I transferred to three different universities. I changed majors again and again. I moved all over the country. I got married and had a baby. Lots of great reasons to lay the book aside until there was more time. (Are you starting to see why it took 16 years?)

Whenever I finally did pick that book up again, I would promise myself, *This time I'm finishing it! No matter what.* But of course, it had been so long since I had looked at it that I had to read it over again from the beginning, just to refamiliarize myself with the content. Can you guess what happened? I'd fall right back into the three-chapter revising loop.

This is Freakout #2. I call him Speedy McRacerpants, which is ironic considering how long you can spend spinning your wheels in his trap. But the thing about Speedy is he's a trickster. He makes you think you're moving forward. You *think* you're doing great. You *think* you're making amazing progress. Sometimes you're even racking up the word count by the tens of thousands. But inevitably, whether it's after three pages or 30,000 words, you go back and read what you wrote.

You never see it coming. You're writing away, feeling good, until one day—BAM! You're staring at a brick wall and you don't know why.

The thing is, you got a little cocky. You escaped the first freakout—the overplanning and outlining stage—and thought you were home free. You were actually writing! Maybe not every single day, but pretty close. The word count rose. The words flowed. You thought, *I got this*, and you started dreaming about the awards you would win and the conferences you'd speak at. Maybe you started a list of podcasts you'd appear on. Everything seemed to be going great.

Then one day, usually somewhere around Chapter 3, Speedy shows up. He just sits there, staring at you as your writing streak comes to a screeching halt and the inevitable self-doubt creeps in.

You read over what you wrote and decide it's not quite right. So you spend a day or two perfecting a couple of rogue paragraphs. No big deal, right? Then you finally realize the REAL trouble with that tricky section. It's not those paragraphs—it's actually the setup for the whole chapter.

So you spend a week (or a month) reworking it. Eventually you decide that chapter is pretty okay, but you want to read it in context. So you go back and read the whole thing from the beginning and…

HOLY CRAP! How could you have been so blind? What you rewrote in Chapter 3 makes *no sense* with Chapters 1 and 2.

You fiddle with it for a few more days before scrapping the whole damn thing and starting the book over from scratch. Or you decide you really need to flesh out your characters, and go down a rabbit hole researching comparative religion for the next six months (or six years).

Your ego is happy. *Technically* you're working on your book. It feels good. You make connections in your brain, have epiphanies, and your dopamine levels go through the roof.

But in reality, you're not writing the book. Speedy has you running in circles. You're writing on tangents. You're procrasti-researching, procrasti-editing, even procrasti-writing. (Yes, even writing can be a procrastination tool to avoid writing. How messed up is that?!)

Like I said, this freakout is tricksy. Because all of those things are important. You need to do them all. The question to ask is: *Do I need to do them right now when I'm supposed to be racking up a word count?*

The procrasti-thingies are actually clever coping mechanisms. Your brain is so smart! You're not procrastinating because you *want* to avoid writing—you're doing everything you know how to *keep* writing. You're trying your best to make progress. (So don't beat yourself up, m'kay?)

The problem is, somewhere along the line you lost your way. And you forgot that you have a map.

Writing is addictive and exciting when the words are flowing. So sometimes Speedy shows up as you're writing off into the sunset on a tangent that really doesn't matter and might even be a whole other book. And sometimes he shows up as doing *anything* tangentially related and calling it writing.

No matter how he shows up, there's a brick wall somewhere in front of you blocking your progress, and you're doing everything you can to avoid looking at it. Because brick walls are scary. They're hard. They hurt when you slam into them.

But this brick wall is your book's best friend. It knows you've strayed from the path that will lead you to The End. It knows where your book is supposed to go, and it just wants you to slow down long enough to take a breath and think for a minute.

Instead of writing and editing in circles trying to avoid the wall, STOP.

Stand right in front of that wall and look at it. Stare it right in the face. Thank it for forcing you to regain your objectivity. Breathe. And remember, you have a map. It was probably the first thing you created. Your outline. Your beat sheet. Or the term I use, your book treatment.

Some would-be authors never make it past this point. Speedy keeps them stuck rewriting the same three chapters forever. Or until they give up on that book and start a new one—a much better one—that also never makes it past the first three chapters.

It took me 16 years to write my first book because of this little bugger. I thought I was making it right, perfect, worthy of publication. But in fact, I was just trapped in front of a brick wall that I didn't know how to get around. So I ignored it and just kept editing. The same three chapters. Like freakin' Groundhog Day!

For that book, I had two strikes against me. First, it was a work of fiction, and I'd never written more than short stories in the past. I'd read a lot of fiction though, so I thought, *How hard could it be to write it?* I had no idea what I was doing.

And because this was a side project, I had no deadlines. That was my second problem. I could write and write, revise, revise, and revise *forever,* and no one would ever call me on it. No one was waiting for it.

A river with no boundaries can't flow—it's just a big mud puddle.

Similarly, a book without deadlines and guidelines may never be finished.

I did finish that first fiction book…16 years later. And it was only because I am *that stubborn!* I decided I was going to finish it no matter what. I eventually recognized my pattern of rewriting the first three chapters and *forced myself* to keep writing and *not look back* until it was finished. I put my outline in front of me and trusted that it would take me all the way to the end of the book.

No rereading or editing in the first draft. That was my new rule. Just follow the map.

During those 16 years of dabbling on that book, I became a journalist and a copywriter. I wrote for clients almost every day. And I stuck religiously to *no editing the first draft until it's done.* I didn't know how valuable that rule was until a lunatic decided it would be a good idea to walk into an elementary school with a gun, and my career changed forever.

The Sandy Hook Elementary School tragedy took the whole country by surprise. The media was full of pundits and experts saying we needed armed guards and metal detectors in every school, that kids should be escorted to the playground by the military. The whole world was screaming, "WE HAVE TO PROTECT THE CHILDREN!" which was true, but the solutions being offered didn't really seem feasible.

At the time, I was writing sales copy for a locksmith who ran a wholesale lock and hardware business. He was a highly respected building security expert. He had consulted on locking hardware and electrified systems for the Olympics, foreign governments, and all branches of the US military. He knew the solution to this problem and was invited to speak on a national radio show about how we could protect the children without traumatizing them or breaking the bank.

"So, Julie, how fast can you write a book?" he asked. Sixteen years seemed like the wrong answer. So I sat there on the phone dumbfounded, trying to figure out how to respond.

"Never mind," he said. "We've got ten days to get one up on Amazon—I know you can do it." And after a short conversation, he hung up.

I did some quick math in my head. They would need at least a few days to turn my words into an actual book.

(I had no idea how to do that back then, or how long it actually took, and neither did my client. Sometimes ignorance can be your best friend.)

I figured I had about a week to write the book he wanted so it would be available when the radio show aired. Whoa! No pressure.

16 YEARS TO 6 DAYS

I didn't have the luxury of freaking out this time. My client was counting on me. Basically, I outran and outwrote the freakouts. But especially Mr. Speedy McRacerpants.

I couldn't let myself write in circles. That's when I figured out why this freakout is so sneaky and how he keeps authors stuck. It's all about our egos. When the book was about something of national importance rather than some fun project I was working on, my ego just didn't matter. It got pushed aside so I could get the work done *fast*.

I think this is the most insidious of all the freakouts, because it can be the hardest trap to escape. The answer comes down to looking at that brick wall and asking…

WTF is this book all about anyway?

What the hell am I trying to say?

Why am I doing this?

What do I want the readers to get out of it?

Unfortunately, these totally legitimate questions manifest in our brains as…

WTF are you doing?

You aren't really a writer.

Everyone's going to find out you don't know what you're talking about.

Better go research sixteenth-century shoe styles before you describe Cinderella getting dressed!

I mostly write nonfiction because, frankly, I think it's easier. Novelists, poets, screenwriters, and playwrights—my hat is off to you! I don't know how you do it. Finding a central theme and weaving it into a satisfying story is an amazing feat.

But for nonfiction, I have a strategy. As a ghostwriter, I have to know certain things before I begin or I will never be able to meet my contracted timelines. Over the years, I figured out the three key elements I *must know* right from the beginning. And as it turns out, these are the same three things that obliterate that brick wall.

Modern drivers have GPS to show them the way; writers have APG.

Audience. Purpose. Goal.

These are the boundaries that turn the stinking mud puddle into a beautiful river that flows wherever you want it to.

When you know your **audience**, you know who you're writing *for*.

Who are they?

What are their problems?

What do they need?

What do they want?

What would make them pick up a book like yours?

Those answers will lead you to the **purpose** of your book.

I like to think of this as moving from Point A to Point B, the beginning to the end. Point A is where your reader is when they pick up your book. They're struggling with a problem. They're stuck in a rut with no direction. They want to be someplace else in their life.

That "someplace else" is Point B. It's where they will end up when they finish your book. They may not have solved the problem completely, but they will have some direction.

And more importantly, they'll have a guide—you.

If you've done a good job writing your book, the reader will trust you to have the answers they seek. If you're a business author, they'll buy your products and programs. They'll use your services. They'll hire you to speak on their stages. They'll donate to your nonprofit.

If you're a fiction author, your character is *definitely* looking to you to take them from Point A to Point B. That journey is the plotline. They have to trust you; they have no choice. You could betray them or not, but you're the boss of your book.

This brings us to the last piece of the puzzle: the **goal**.

What's in it for you as the author?

What do you get out of the deal?

Writing a book is a huge undertaking. If there's nothing in it for you personally—no reward for all that work—you'll find it almost impossible to finish. You'll give up before the end. Freakout #2 will defeat you.

Back in the day, the goal was simply to get published, because that alone was a huge reward. But with all the advances in self and hybrid publishing, that goal is no longer enough. Anyone can get published. It's easy. But not just anyone can write a good book.

So you need a bigger goal to keep you going when things get dicey. If audience and purpose are the riverbanks that keep the words flowing in the right direction, your goal is the third boundary, the riverbed. And you get to *choose* where it leads.

The reason Speedy traps us into running in circles is because we get caught up in what *we* want to say, rather than what the reader needs to know. Our egos trip us up. We stop following the map. And when we lose our way, we tend to be stubborn and not ask for directions.

Now I'm not saying you should never abandon your outline—that can and should be a fluid document. But your audience, purpose, and goal should be fixed. They form your North Star, your guiding light. If you're unsure about a story, a framework, an exercise, or an example, ask yourself, "Does this align with my audience, purpose, and goal?"

If yes, keep it.

If no, it probably belongs in another book.

Let's say you're writing a weight-loss book and you want to include a story about losing your job and starting over in a brand-new career at 45. Does that story fit? Let's check for alignment with the APG.

If the story is a completely random little bit of personal trivia, it probably doesn't belong. On the other hand, if you're talking about how stress and cortisol affect people's weight, and the story illustrates a time you were stressed out and struggled with the scale, then it should stay.

In fiction, just ask yourself whether a particular scene actually moves the story forward in some way. Does it provide insight into a character and their motivations? Does it move the action forward? Does it resolve or complicate? If yes, keep it. If no, cut it.

If it "sort of" works, maybe it should be used as supplementary material like an appendix or a bonus download from your website. If you're not sure, just mark it as something to look at in the second-draft phase and keep moving forward. Keep writing. Don't look back.

Important Note: Sometimes the problem is not about endless editing in circles. Sometimes it's about you writing your butt off and being so excited about what a great writer you are that you are 100,000 words into your draft before you realize it has *nothing* to do with your original intention. Once again, your ego has trapped you into making the book all about *you* and how smart you are instead of keeping the focus on the reader.

The solution here is the same. Go back to your audience, purpose, and goal. Does what you've written align? Or have you been writing a completely different book?

WHAT'S THE GIFT OF FREAKOUT #2?

Speedy's gift is commitment. You *are* going to see this through to the end. When you learn to recognize when you're off course and need to use your map, you will end up with a book that lands with its intended audience and produces the desired result.

You've probably read books that were terrible in your opinion, right? So what went wrong? Were you the intended audience or not? If you were—and the book didn't deliver on its promise—then the author likely never defined their audience, purpose, and goal early in the planning stages.

Overcoming this freakout pulls you back out of your ego and puts the focus where it belongs—on the *hero*. This is either the protagonist or the reader, depending on your book.

Overcoming Freakout #2 also gifts you with results for *yourself*—meaning you'll actually finish the book you intended to write and (hopefully) meet the goals you set for yourself.

Your audience, purpose, and goal. That's your map. You just forgot for a moment, that's all. When you're able to remember who you're writing for, what you're trying to convey, and why, you'll find that brick wall crumbles and disappears like magic. You stop running in circles and start making actual progress.

Now there's a lot of writing ahead of you before you get to Freakout #3. The whole book, in fact. So be very aware that Speedy can trap you at any time. You have the map though. Anytime you catch yourself editing something over and over, anytime you're not sure you're on the right track, pull out your APG and do an alignment check.

I tell my students to write them on an index card and tape it to their computers. Put it where you'll see it every day. Your map is your *best friend*.

Now it's time to write. And write and write and write and write some more. (*God this is tedious—will it ever end?*) Don't stop. Keep writing. I know it's exhausting sometimes, but you have to keep pushing forward until one day—BAM!

That's it! You're actually finished with your first draft.

WOOOO-HOOOO!!!

Take a moment to enjoy your accomplishment. Really savor it. You wrote a first-pass manuscript. Most people who start a book never get this far. Throw yourself a nice celebration dinner. Get a massage. Take a day off.

Just don't break out the really expensive champagne yet—you're about to step into the clutches of the third author freakout.

AUTHOR FREAKOUT #3
SIGH JUSTSIGH

The End.

Yes! I did it! WOOO-HOOO!

Break out the celebratory vat of ice cream because my book is finished! I didn't think I'd ever make it to the finish line. I wanted to quit so many times, but I am disciplined and awesome. And I feel so BADASS right now!!

That's the scene that replays in my mind every time I finish a draft.

If you haven't reached that point yet, consider it a preview. There is *nothing* like finishing the first draft of a book you've poured your heart and soul and time into. It's a major accomplishment. You deserve to celebrate in whatever way you choose.

At this point, it's tempting to believe the voices in your head telling you that all the manuscript needs is a quick brushup and it will be ready to publish. (Or worse, that it's ready to go immediately.)

Do not believe the voices in your head. You're about to meet Freakout #3, Sigh.

I always advise my clients and students to let their first drafts sit for about two weeks. The words need to marinate. They need time to get to know each other and decide if they like each other.

The author needs to step back too. Because we are WAY too close to our books. We need to regain perspective. Our words are not our babies; they are just words. And those words must either stay or go based on ruthless objectivity and adherence to the audience, purpose, and goal.

There's no better way to gain that necessary perspective than spending some time away from your manuscript.

That said, you don't want to lose the precious momentum you've built up. Your carefully cultivated writing routine can easily fall to pieces if you spend too much time away from it. Instead, consider that break a great time to do other book-related activities like making a publishing plan, getting a cover design (if you're self-publishing), and starting your marketing. (It's never too early to start marketing your book, no matter who's publishing it.)

When you're ready to come back to your first draft, you might be tempted to think you're home free. Just a few tweaks and it'll be ready to publish.

I can't tell you how many authors come to me with a manuscript that "just needs a little cleaning up" when in reality, it's a hot mess.

In the immortal words of Winston Churchill, "Now this is not the end. It is not even the beginning of the end. But it is, perhaps, the end of the beginning." The more chuffed you are about your first draft, the more susceptible you may be to Sigh's trap.

HE SHOWS UP WHEN YOU READ THROUGH YOUR FIRST DRAFT...AND YOU HATE IT.

(This space intentionally left blank for proper emotional response and possible crying fit…)

It absolutely sucks.

What were you thinking?

What a waste of time and energy!

Who do you think you are trying to write a book anyway?

You may have a milder reaction and simply be underwhelmed by your work. Either way, Sigh's strategy is to make you justify giving up at this point. You might think things like…

Nobody reads books anymore.

It's just a business card. It doesn't matter if it's any good.

This is my practice book. It's okay if it's not great. The next one will be better.

You've already put in so much time. You thought you were writing exactly what needed to be said. You were *trying your best*. So if you're not jazzed about the outcome, you should probably just give up on this writing thing, right?

This is a critical juncture in your journey. It's the dark night of the soul for our hero. (That's you!) It's the time you'll be most tempted to let your book just slip away from you.

How you handle Sigh and the words he whispers in your ear can make the difference between becoming a published author and never finishing your book.

At this point, you're being called to make a decision. There are a few ways you could handle the disappointment.

- You could decide you're not meant to be a writer after all, give up, and move on. Honestly, for some people, this isn't a terrible thing to do. At least it frees them from the trap—and the guilt—even if it doesn't get them a book in the end.

- You could decide that this particular book was never meant to be, go back to the drawing board, and start a new one. It's a very popular option, and also not a bad plan for some books. Just remember that you'll still have to face Sigh again when you finish drafting the new manuscript.

- You could decide to publish it as is—a popular option with so many business writers, but definitely *NOT* recommended. No rough draft is ready to be published as is.

- You could decide to get professional help—either from a developmental editor, a book coach, or a ghostwriter.

All good options if you find the right match and are willing to pay for their expertise.

- You could decide to tackle your hot mess of a manuscript head-on and fix it, no matter how long it takes.

You simply have to choose the option you believe will lead you to a book you can be proud of. Which option will serve your audience best?

Unfortunately, many authors decide not to do anything at all. They decide not to make a decision. They abdicate the throne. They put the manuscript away thinking, *Phew! I did it. I wrote the book. It's all downhill from here. All I have to do is clean it up a bit and it'll be done.*

And then what happens?

Nothing.

That first draft might sit in the dark for *decades* and never see the light of day again. Why? Because the author is so "busy."

We all have a million things tugging at our attention. We did the hard work already, and *as soon as this current thing is over, we'll get right back to the book.*

As soon as this business crisis is over…

As soon as the kids are on summer break…

As soon as things slow down…

Guess what? Things never slow down.

The longer your manuscript sits, the more guilt will build up inside you for abandoning the project. For giving up halfway through. For not making it a priority. The longer you let it sit, the less chance it has of ever being published.

If you want to make it to the end of the journey, you have to keep your book a top priority. You have to continue looking at it, even when it's painful. Keep playing with it. Keep tweaking it until it's ready for editing.

Don't let all your hard work be for nothing. Don't let Sigh win.

You might be thinking, *Well, that's all fine and dandy, Julie, but what if I don't love it and don't know how to fix it? I gave it my best shot, and it's not great. Why shouldn't I give up?*

Because you're exactly where you're supposed to be!

You haven't done anything wrong. It's called a rough draft for a reason.

The good news is there is no limit to how rough your rough draft can be. (Someone brilliant said that. It's a meme.)

As long as you've written down your thoughts, you're good. Your draft can be full of holes and half-completed sentences. It can have huge gaps with notations like {research this}. It's allowed to be a hot mess, as long as you expect it and don't let fear of the work ahead stop you in your tracks.

The trap is thinking that your work will be mostly done once you type "The End" the first time.

If you prepare yourself and don't expect your first draft to be a work of art, Sigh will have less of an effect. He may be able to plant the seeds of doom and gloom, but you won't spend as much time spinning out in your brain. The self-doubt won't be able to take hold, because you're *expecting* to be let down a bit by your work. And you know that the letdown doesn't mean you won't wind up with a brilliant book. It simply means you have more work to do.

And you know what? You might actually be surprised by how *good* some parts of your book are. You might even think, *Damn, I can actually write. This bit right here—it's awesome!* Hold tight to those thoughts. They will keep you going.

If self-doubt does have you spinning around in your head, or if you can physically feel the emotions as tightness in your chest or a sickly feeling in your gut, it's time to get a second opinion before you make any rash decisions.

Do *not* give the manuscript to your mother or your favorite uncle or anyone who will just tell you what you want to hear. Find a developmental editor, another author, or someone you trust to give you a solid opinion of your work.

Did you ever have a teacher or mentor who just seemed mean? Someone who was tough on you and wouldn't let you get away with anything?

I had a history teacher in high school like that—Mrs. Sanborn. You couldn't coast in her class. You had to be engaged in discussion and actually think. She challenged us. Everyone hated her class when they were going through it. Freshmen were told horror stories about Modern European History and how hard it was.

But then somehow she magically morphed into the best teacher we ever had (*after* we were through the class).

That's the kind of person you want on your side. Every hero needs a guide to show them the way through the forest and make sure they don't give up. (And to kick their butt into gear from time to time.)

Freakout #3 is the easiest to spot because he shows up right on schedule. Reading your first draft? Feeling kinda down about it? There he is. But the truth is, he's like that tough teacher in high school. It only *seems* like he hates you and wants you to fail. That's the trap. In reality, he's a big marshmallow. He'll give you the clothes off his back, if you'll just keep going.

He wants you to see that you're not finished yet—there's more of you to give. And your readers deserve your best effort.

He wants you to see that you are the boss of your book, and you have the power to change the words to suit your purpose. When you look at Sigh Justsigh through the lens of compassion and cut yourself some slack, you'll see he is offering you the gift of CONTROL.

One of my favorite clients, Russell, was working on his second book with me. His first one had been a huge hit, propelling his company past the eight-figure mark, and he wanted his second one to be just as good. (This is often called the sophomore slump, where you're afraid your first book was a fluke.)

Freakout #3 hit him hard. He didn't talk to me or answer my messages for months. I started to wonder if he'd fallen off the planet!

But the truth was that he was underwhelmed with his book, and he couldn't quite put his finger on why. He wrestled with it, prayed over it, and showed it to trusted colleagues. At the end of the day, it was just the wrong book. It wasn't what he wanted to say at all. When he finally realized that and accepted that he would have to start over, he did two things:

1. He went live on Snapchat and pressed Delete in front of the whole world! Like, he just nuked his entire manuscript.

2. He messaged me and said, "Don't hate me! But I have a much better idea..."

And he did. The concepts and frameworks that came out of the revision process have literally helped shape the modern business world. That second book, *Expert Secrets*, has helped hundreds of thousands of people build all kinds of incredible businesses. And it solidified Russell's place as a globally impactful leader.

Most of the time, you don't have to go to such dramatic lengths to fix your manuscript. But sometimes the nuclear option is the right one. So much of the publishing process will feel out of your control. But as for the words—only YOU decide when they're just right.

Treat your revision period as sacred space. This is your time to experiment and play with your words. You can cut, paste, research, add, subtract, shift around. You can add pictures and graphs. You can envision new frameworks and subplots.

Right now, I'm revising this chapter for the third time. I'm trying to put myself in your shoes. I'm trying to get into the same emotional state you'll be in when you're dancing with Sigh.

I'm trying to make it just right. For you, dear reader. Because you matter to me. And I can't wait to read your book.

You're the boss. You're in control. Take as long as you need.

There's no limit to the number of times you can comb through your manuscript…

…until there is.

At some point, your revisions must be complete. Eventually, you have to move to the next stage and hand your work off to someone else: The Editor (dun, dun, **duuuuun**).

Enter Freakout #4, right on schedule.

AUTHOR FREAKOUT #4
PERCIVAL VONPERFECT IV

Just one more tweak to Chapter 3.

No wait…I think it needs to move in front of Chapter 8. Ooh, what about an appendix? I think it just needs one more read-through.

Wait! This book will make so much more sense if I write this other book first. Let me get to work on that one…

For CRYING OUT LOUD!

Percival (or Percy, for short) will have you chasing your tail forever if he can. Because it's time to turn your baby over to the experts who will make it into a "real book." And if you're self-publishing, he's even more troublesome, because you have to switch between author mode and publisher mode over and over until it's just right.

At some point, you have to be done.

Done revising.

Done reordering.

Done getting feedback from beta readers.

At some point, you have to turn in your work.

And that takes trust.

You have to trust that your editor and publisher have your book's best interests at heart. If you're self-publishing, you might not even know who you need on your team to help you. It's possible you're planning to get your cousin Louise to edit your book. (She's got a degree in creative writing, after all.)

Think about the last time you had to "turn in your work." It was probably high school or college, yes? And there was a grade attached, which means someone was going to *judge* it and decide whether it was acceptable or not. So naturally you wanted to make the piece the best that you possibly could. This is exactly what Percy loves—that place of "not good enough" and "I can make it better."

Perfectionism.

Percy shows up as an endless revision cycle. You're just never quite ready to send it off to editing and production. At least in school you had a deadline to meet. And if you're being traditionally published, you might still have the luxury of a hard deadline. Without it, this little guy can keep you wrapped up in your own head for weeks, months, or forever.

Even veteran authors feel this twinge of uncertainty when it's time to turn in their work. It feels a little like sending your child off to their first day of school. Will the teacher be nice? Will they know how to handle your precious baby's special needs? What if your book comes back and you don't recognize it?

Here's the thing—if you don't trust your publisher, get another one.

If you don't know who to hire to edit and lay out your self-published book, find a guide. Because sooner or later, you're going to have to let go. And handling the entire publishing process by yourself is rarely the right thing to do.

You need outside perspective. You need other people to help you move the project forward. And it really helps if you have a load of preorders, so you know people are expecting the book by a certain date. (You did start your marketing early, right?)

Here are a few facts every soon-to-be author needs to know and every veteran author should remember.

You will have more than one round of edits. Your work doesn't have to be 100% perfect right now. When that manuscript comes back all marked up, you might be tempted to trash the whole thing and start over. But that's the time to buckle down and get the final tweaks complete. And you won't be guessing at what needs adjusting; you'll have professional guidance.

Book people love books and they want yours to succeed. Editors, designers, and publishers all love what they do. If they didn't, they wouldn't be in this industry. There are far more lucrative ways to make a living. They want your book to be presented in the best possible way. They know the book business. They understand what book buyers want and expect. Allow them to help you turn your beautiful creation into something even more amazing.

I've worked with a lot of authors as their coach, ghostwriter, or publisher, and they all start out resisting suggested changes. But once the book is published, they concede that the book is better because of the additional input and expertise.

Honest feedback is important. Sometimes feedback stings. Sometimes it's not all puppies and rainbows and "OMG, this book is FANTASTIC!" We authors put so much time and effort into the writing that any outside criticism can feel like an attack, even the really small stuff like passive voice and tense changes.

I know you love your words. We all do. But learn to take the not-so-great feedback gracefully. You don't have to change anything because of an editor or beta reader's comments, but you owe it to your book to at least consider whether that person might be on to something really fantastic.

You are the boss of your book. Occasionally, an editor or publishing team will make a suggestion that you just don't want to accept. They might suggest that the cover is *all wrong* or that they dislike the interior layout. Or the editor might have made a mess of your prose by completely changing your voice.

At the end of the day, you are the boss of your book. That means you should always have the final say. In traditional publishing, that may not be the case. But even with an ironclad contract, your publisher should be open to your feedback and desires.

When you're in the throes of Freakout #4, it's time to get focused on the final result. Do you want your book published or not? Are you nitpicking little details and fighting your publishing team because those details matter? Or are you micromanaging because Percy is in control and stalling the project? Total self-awareness is called for here.

Is there any part of you, deep down, that doesn't want this project to move forward to completion? Maybe the part of you that just loves playing around with ideas. Or the part of you that enjoys having something important and creative *all to yourself.* Or the part that's afraid of hearing another Uncle Arthur lecture from your mom.

What would be the payoff if you just kept tweaking and adjusting forever? Maybe you'd get to keep that feeling of "my book is almost ready and the world is going to love it" instead of risking possible rejection by actually putting it out into the world.

I find the best thing is to take a deep breath, send the manuscript to your publisher, and get busy doing other work to help ensure the project is a success. Take your mind off the fact that other people are reading and evaluating your work. Here are some things you can do to keep busy while your manuscript is in production.

- Work on your launch marketing.
- Build your platform/following.
- Create supplemental materials.
- Build a sales funnel.
- Start an email list.
- Create social media graphics.
- Start writing your next book.

When you overcome Percy's trap, you get the gift of confidence. Surrendering your book to the expertise of others means you've learned trust. And when you see that they really do have your book's best interests at heart, you are able to move forward, confident that the work will be better than you could ever could have made it by yourself.

One of my favorite parts of any book is the acknowledgements section. Sometimes I even read them before the main content. Acknowledgements are the author's thank-you note to Freakout #4. They show that *no book* is created in a vacuum. No author is solely responsible for their creation. It takes an army of people all supporting the author, pushing the project forward.

Acknowledgements usually thank three groups of people.

- The family and friends who supported the author physically, emotionally, and sometimes financially during the long journey of writing the book

- The mentors, teachers, and colleagues who helped the author form their thoughts, ideas, and philosophies over time

- The editors, writers, designers, publisher, and other support people who handled the production details

Allow these people to support you. No book is an island. It is a labor of love that requires trust in others. If you let Percival VonPerfect keep you trapped, your book will never be fully formed. It will forever be an almost-book.

Only you can decide when you're ready to see Percy for who he really is—a foolish notion that your ideas aren't actually ready to be a "real book" or that you aren't ready to be an author. At some point, you have to stop revising and tweaking and fixing. At some point, you have to trust others to take the project the rest of the way.

Here's the thing—you are an ever-evolving creature. You learn and grow. Your ideas change. And because of this, you could revise and tweak and fix your manuscript forever and it would *never* be finished.

A book is a static thing. It doesn't grow and change once it's printed. It is permanent. And in an ever-changing digital world where *nothing* is permanent, that can be terrifying. However, it's exactly that permanence in an impermanent world that gives books their gravitas and value. That's what makes them special.

Recognize that a book is a moment in time. It's a snapshot of ideas and thoughts and attitudes at one time in your life. You will continue to grow and evolve; your book will not. You and your book will part ways. It will remain at a certain point in time to help others who are in that same place. Your book is a gift to those people.

Once you are satisfied that you've captured your ideas in words, you can stop. Put down your pen (or, you know, close your computer) and let others pick up the project and carry it across the finish line. You are allowed to finish. It is safe to complete.

There's one more freakout to go. And this one can last for years, even after your book has been officially released.

AUTHOR FREAKOUT #5
PLEASY WORTHINGTON

When did you learn to hide your words?

When did you decide it wasn't safe to be seen or heard?

Who laughed at your stories, ridiculed your thoughts, or graded and judged your papers?

In other words…

When did you decide it *wasn't safe* to write or share your writing?

I was 16 when I finally closed and locked the door on my writing. It wasn't safe—emotionally or physically—to risk *anyone* seeing what I wrote. Or at least not anything that I truly felt. My authentic voice was shut away.

The circumstances don't really matter. Suffice it to say that a close family authority figure read my private journal, where I had placed my most vulnerable thoughts and feelings. Where I was just learning to express how I actually felt. He violated that sacred space. And some really terrible stuff happened to me because of what he read.

I'm now 53, and it was just a little while ago that I figured out what had happened. I understand now what I did to protect myself from the hurt, anger, and shame. I finally see that I have been hiding my words since that moment. I've been swallowing the truth and burying it deep inside me for the sake of peace and safety.

"But Julie, you've been a professional writer for thirty years! What are you talking about? Writing is your whole career." That's true.

I've been a reporter.

I've been a copywriter.

I've been a ghostwriter.

I've been a writing coach and editor.

I've been a publisher.

Can you spot the pattern?

Other. People's. Words.

Someone. Else's. Story.

Never my own.

I've written my own books, sure. But I've never put them out into the world in a big way. I never really advertised them. They were "practice books"—never intended for the whole world to see them.

Clever me. I found a way to write but still stay hidden and safe. All because I made up a story when I was 16 that it wasn't safe to let others read my words.

This is Freakout #5. And it is the most terrible, I think, because it can last days, months, years, or *your entire life* if you let it.

If you've written, edited, and published your book but it's not selling as well as you'd hoped…

Or you're holding back on launching, marketing, and *selling* your book…

Ask yourself why.

Is it because you lack financial resources?

Is it because you're not good at selling?

Is it because you don't know how to market?

These are perfectly legit excuses that Freakout #5 puts in our heads.

And they are lies.

They are stories we choose to believe in order to feel safe. Because at some point we learned it wasn't safe to share our writing with the world. It wasn't safe to be seen or heard.

That is the root of the problem. That is where you need to look for answers. Because if you can find the incident in your past that's still haunting you, you can shine a light on that sucker. You can see it for what it really is and request that it kindly take its freakin' foot *off the brake!*

It's possible this freakout isn't rooted in your own past. Maybe you've just heard horror stories in your online writers' groups, and that was enough to subconsciously put your foot on the brake. Maybe you watched someone else's words get ripped to shreds. Maybe you saw how much that writer was hurt and decided that was *never* going to happen to you.

I call this freakout Pleasy. As in *Please like me!* He can be a minor irritation, just a little nervousness around your book's release date as you think, *I hope people like it.* Or as in my case, he can be the root cause of a whole lot of frustration (for, like, most of my life).

If you have a traditional publisher, you probably won't be able to physically stop the release of your book. But Pleasy can minimize your efforts to get the word out. He will make darn sure you don't post about your book. Or create a marketing plan. Or actually execute your marketing plans.

Instead you'll let your book quietly die and then listen to Pleasy say...

> *See? Nobody liked it. Nobody bought it. That's because you're not ready. You're not good enough. Better try again on a new project. Better yet, give up writing altogether. I hear badminton is fun. Or maybe take up knitting...*

Ugh.

If you didn't do your best to put your book out there, why not?

Is it possible you really don't know how to market yourself? (A quick Google search on "book marketing" will show you how.)

Or is there something deeper you need to uncover? Possibly something painful? Something you locked away a long time ago?

If there *is* something else, then no amount of marketing, reviews, or money spent will result in a successful book. Because your subconscious will block it by stomping on the brake.

You will subconsciously negate your own best efforts. You *will* stay safe. Even if your conscious mind wants nothing more than to sell thousands of copies. You can't defeat a strong Freakout #5 until you believe that it's 100% safe to be successful.

You must be willing for people to see you and read your words. And yes, you must be willing to let them judge your work. Because that's going to happen. But you don't have to allow their words to affect you. Feel the sting if you must, but don't let it penetrate and get under your skin. Let it go. Robin Sharma said, "Other people's opinions are none of your business." That's great advice and really hard to follow for many people.

Since you're a writer, journaling on a few questions is probably the best way to uncover what's actually going on. You can noodle them in your head, but that's where the freakouts hang out, so it's probably best not to *think* through this.

Instead, I invite you to *feel* through this.

Get quiet, connect to your heart, and have an honest conversation with the child inside you. You know, the one who's really running the show right now. Because she's scared and just wants to stay safe. And right now, as an almost-author, you are safe.

Here's how you defeat Pleasy, whether you're getting ready to release your book or it's been published for a while.

1. Go someplace private and bring a journal with you. Writing by hand is going to be more effective than typing.

2. Close your eyes and retreat inside yourself. Try to find that child. She's probably somewhere in your heart region, but she could be someplace else in your body. She has the answers you seek. She knows the real reason your books aren't as successful as you want them to be. She knows the secret belief that's blocking your marketing efforts.

3. Gently ask her a few questions like…

   How are you feeling right now?

   Do you feel safe writing our books?

   Do you feel safe letting strangers read and judge our books?

   How would you feel if we were a massively successful author?

4. Listen. *Really listen* to what she says. In fact, write it down *word-for-word*. Even if what you're writing doesn't make any sense right away. Let her take as long as she needs to speak. She might be *really* scared to say what she truly feels. She might want to talk about something totally unrelated. Or she might not want to talk at all.

Be patient.

5. When she does answer, ask follow-up questions to understand what kind of stories and beliefs she/you have around writing, words, voice, and success.

    Why do you think you feel that way? When did you first start feeling that way?

    When did you learn to believe that? What made you decide that?

    What would change your mind?

    Is there anything I can do to help you feel safe?

    What do you really want from me?

    She's probably going to answer you with the very beliefs that are holding you back. If you pay close attention, you'll know the truth when you hear it. Something will jump out at you or seem more significant than everything else you're writing down. You might even feel tears welling up inside you. That's a clue that you're on the right track.

6. Once you find the issues, it's time to gently shift her point of view. Go back to your reasons for not putting your books out into the world and ask,

    "Is this true or is it fear? And if it is actually fear—what might I be afraid of?"

7. If you uncover fears, again ask, "Is that true? What can I do to mitigate them?"

Like this.

Why do you think our book isn't selling?

Because I'm lousy at sales.

Is that true?

Well, not really. I've never actually tried it.

Is that because you're afraid to try?

Maybe.

What are you afraid of?

I don't want to come across as a used-car salesperson.

Hypothetically, how could you get around that and still sell books?

Well, maybe I could read some book marketing blogs and learn a few non-salesy ways to promote my book. I could reframe how I think about sales.

That sounds like a great idea! Is it okay if we do that? Just read a few articles? Would that be safe?

Yes, I think we could do that.

Thank you for working with me on this. I think we make a great team!

BOOM! You just won her over…for the first step anyway. You will need to consult her again when it's time to implement what you've learned by reading those articles.

Maybe the conversation would sound something like this:

So I like this idea of being a guest on a few podcasts. What do you think about that?

I don't know. What if we can't think of anything to say? What if we make fools of ourselves?

Well, that's certainly a risk. But we could find a really nice host. Someone who will help us along. It's really just answering questions. I think we could do it.

Well, we do know a lot about our topic. We wrote a book about it, after all.

Exactly. What if we try it out with just one podcast, just to see if we like it. We don't have to do any more if we don't want to. Would that feel safe?

Just one? Yes, I think I could do that.

Great! I promise to check in with you after it's done. I think we're going to have fun!

Me too!

You're getting her buy-in a little at a time. Better yet, you're learning how to connect with her anytime you need to. If you open regular conversations with that little angel, you might find she's got tons of great ideas. She has the answers you seek. All you have to do is ask the right questions and *really listen*.

You might strike gold with your first conversation, or you might not even be able to locate someone to talk to. That's okay—keep trying.

Sometimes we've ignored our inner child so long, she's angry with us and has no reason to want to talk to us. And you're on her turf. You need to win her trust before she will listen to what you have to say. Ultimately, you want her to take her foot off the brake and come over to your side.

Send your inner child plenty of love and acceptance. Don't tell her she's crazy or wrong, or blame her for holding you back. Bullying her is only going to make her dig in harder. This is your *self* you're talking to. Be gentle, even if it feels weird. Love her. Accept her where she is. Praise her for coming up with such a brilliant story and keeping you both safe all these years.

Explain to her that you really want your books to be out in the world. Tell her why. You want to help people overcome problems. Or you want your stories to make people laugh. Show her that the rewards will be worth the risks.

Validate her fears. Yes, some people might not like what we say. It's true, we can't control bad reviews or online trolls. But they are so few and far between. And if they ever hurt her, what will you do to make it better? Will you take her out for ice cream? Will you cry with her in a one-hour pity party and then call a trusted friend to make it better? Make a plan with your inner child that makes her feel like she can release her grip on whatever's keeping you stuck.

You may have heard advice like "Align your head and your heart" or "All parts of you need to be on the same page." That's your goal with this exercise. You're clearing up any and all objections, stories, and negative beliefs that might be lingering in your subconscious.

And guess what? It might take some time. That's okay. You might need to take baby steps. That's okay too. Get your inner child to agree to sharing your book with friends on social media. Or placing an ad on Amazon, just for a few days. Or setting up an email list so people can join if they want to.

Lots of things can happen when you go through this exercise. You might cry. You might laugh. You might get royally pissed off at something that happened decades ago when you realize *that one stupid event* has affected your entire life. It's important to let those emotions bubble up and out of you. That's the only way to fully release what's blocking you from putting yourself out there.

I carefully crafted a successful and safe 30-year career of writing other people's words. Other people's stories. Using my genius to help other people shine. And I was really good at it. (I still am!)

But until I uncovered the truth that it wasn't safe to share my own writing—my own truth—I couldn't get past writing basic how-to information.

I couldn't even manage to write an email to my list unless it was giving away information.

Sharing insights? *Nope.*

Challenging assumptions? *Uh-uh.*

Getting vulnerable? *Oh HELL no!*

The reason Freakout #5 can be so powerful is because you're giving up control. Once you start marketing your book, you have no control over who might read it. And you have no control over what they might say. Or how they might react.

Or how they might *HURT YOU.*

The deeper you were hurt by someone else's reaction to your writing in the past, the worse Pleasy can be.

But here's the thing—read any book on publishing or marketing creative work and you'll find the same advice over and over. Some people just aren't going to like your book. They might be triggered by something you say. They might have an opposing viewpoint. They may feel confronted and may not be ready to change their own behavior or beliefs—so they lash out at you.

You have no control over what people say. So don't attach yourself to outside comments or reviews. Yes, they can sting. Trolls and meanies thrive on inflicting pain. It fuels their sick egos.

But you DO have control over how you react to other people's comments. Total strangers might make negative comments about your book, but that doesn't mean you have to take them personally. They might say it lacks depth or meaning. But that doesn't mean *you* lack depth. They don't even know you.

And you are not your book.

Also, when it comes to emotional pain, no one can hurt you without your consent.

Let me say that again.

When it comes to emotional pain, *no one can hurt you without your consent.*

Unless some part of you *agrees* (or expects) to be hurt by bad reviews or snarky comments, they have no power over you.

Have you ever said something nasty to someone and they just didn't care? They gave no reaction at all? It doesn't happen very often, because we live in such a reactive society. Our entire economy is run on the fact that we allow others to control and manipulate how we feel from moment to moment.

But what if the comments just bounced off you and never affected you for a second?

Of course you care about what people think of your book. You want the world to like it and buy lots of copies. But what would happen if you weren't *attached* to that? What if you could accept praise and scorn with the same objective emotion?

What if you loved your work so much that other people's opinions just didn't matter?

Would you be able to market your book without fear of being hurt? Would it be safe for others to read your words?

It sounds overly simple, but all you have to do is *decide*. Make the conscious decision that you're not going to play the game. You're withdrawing consent to allow anyone to hurt you with their opinion of your writing. You're giving people permission to believe whatever they want about your book, and you don't have to react to it at all.

That decision does two things.

1. It puts you firmly in control of your emotions and feelings. You reclaim your power—your power of choice in how you react to anything that happens.

2. It cuts the cord attaching you to your book, which allows that book to go out into the world and do its job.

Your words have magic in them. If you wrote that book with intention, then it has stories to tell and work to do. Work that it can only do if you allow it to be seen. Repeat after me:

> *It is safe for people to read my words.*
>
> *No one has power over me without my consent.*

When you can say those sentences without feeling triggered, you are free of Pleasy's trap. And that means you get to collect his gift: contribution.

Ultimately, every author starts writing because they want to make a contribution. And when you escape the trap of hiding your words, your book can make its greatest contribution and do its job in the world. (Like this one you're reading right now. I wonder how it's doing. I hope it's helping tons of people.)

She really is a genius, you know. Your inner child. She will help you through this if you let her. In fact, if you start talking to her right from the very beginning of a book project, she can help you through all the frustrating bits. You can be the world's greatest power team!

IT'S TOOL TIME

Your freakouts have been with you all along. They've helped you procrastinate. They've carefully planted seeds of self-doubt and encouraged imposter syndrome. They've firmly kept their collective foot on the brake of your subconscious mind. But no more! You're on to their sneaky ways. You know when they're going to show up and why. You even know a few tricks to convince them to see things your way.

Now it's time to arm yourself, to "screw your courage to the sticking place," as Lady Macbeth would say. Because you're about to learn five tools that will not only keep the freakouts out of your way, but will also uncover the limiting beliefs that have been running the show.

It takes courage to face some of the shadows lurking deep in your subconscious mind. But it's worth every effort you can make for a couple of reasons.

- Once you uncover those limiting beliefs, you can change them. Which means your whole life can improve even though all you were trying to do was finish your book.

- Once you understand more about your own subconscious blocks and resistance, just imagine how much better your writing will be! Your characters will come alive with nuance and emotion. Your plotlines will dance. Human behavior will be easier to explain. (How cool is that?!)

These tools can be used anytime to handle any freakout. You may have a favorite that you use all the time. Or you might try them all out to see which one works on a particularly stubborn freakout. I didn't invent these tools. I merely applied them to the writing craft.

Enjoy!

TOOL #1

CONVERSATIONS
WITH A FREAKOUT

You're going to be so good at this one! Grab a notebook and two different color pens. Talk to the freakout using one color, and let him talk back in a different one. Ask him questions. Try to understand his point of view. But do *not* agree with that point of view. There's a difference. Don't let the freakout convince you it's right. You are stronger than your freakout. You are the boss.

As you go through this exercise, your freakout will tell you exactly where your beliefs are holding you back. As it's talking, remember you have the power to agree or disagree with it. If you agree with it, you'll stay stuck. If you see through it for the BS it actually is, you'll be free.

If you're facing a particularly nasty freakout, you might need to write for a while. Or you might need to have several conversations with it before you can shift it. That's okay. It's a writing exercise—you're good at this.

What you're really doing here is letting your conscious mind talk to your subconscious mind. You're unearthing deeply held beliefs that are holding you back or sabotaging your work. You're discovering where you have one foot on the brake.

Your goal with the exercise is to get the freakout to verbally agree that he is wrong and you are right. In other words, that the limiting or sabotaging belief is not actually true. You might need to scream at the freakout by writing in all caps. You might need to sweet-talk it. If one tactic doesn't work, try another.

These beliefs are the programming you've been carrying around since you were very young. The more firmly you hold those beliefs, the more he will argue back when you use this exercise. Let him speak.

He will appeal to your likes and dislikes. He will sound convincing. He will tell you exactly what the procrastinator inside you wants to hear. In other words, he'll lie. And since this is a conversation happening in your own mind…well, it's tricky. You have to practice this. It might take a few tries to *really* connect with this part of you.

There are signs that you've gotten through to the little bugger. You might feel a tightness in your throat or chest. You might cry a little (or a LOT). You might feel intense rage or shame. These are good! Powerful emotions mean you're tapping into the source of the freakout.

You might feel a bit schizophrenic with multiple voices talking at once. That's okay. Giving voice to your subconscious is one of the most empowering things you can do for yourself.

You might be surprised to hear your mother's or father's voice in the words the freakout uses. That's not a coincidence. And again, it's okay. Just let it keep talking. Then allow your best self to refute every argument it comes up with.

And one more thing—don't be surprised if you discover that the belief goes deeper than your writing. It might be running your entire life—affecting your finances, your health, your relationships. When you recognize those patterns, celebrate! Every time you consciously choose to shift a limiting belief or negative pattern, life starts to get easier.

Here's a short example. Most conversations with my freakouts span many pages!

I see you, freakout. What are you up to in there? You know I'm trying to get an outline started for this book. Why are you making me question my decisions?

Well you see, it's just that you're so smart! You have such a huge responsibility to save your readers from themselves. I'm just helping you make sure everything you write is perfect.

It's true. I am smart. And that's why I can see through your games. The truth is it's actually NOT my responsibility to save my readers. They can only do that themselves. I can only guide them with a few ideas and strategies that have worked for me. What they do from there is on them. Wouldn't you agree?

Umm…I guess so.

And as far as making everything I write perfect, well we both know that's impossible. There's no such thing as perfect, because no two people see things in exactly the same way. Isn't that right?

That's true.

So basically, you've got me spinning in circles in the hopes of achieving something that's actually impossible. You're not helping; you're keeping me from moving

forward with this outline. You're making me second-guess everything I type. I don't need to be perfect right now. There's time for that later. At this very moment, I need to be in motion! Yes?

Fine…yes.

Wonderful. I'm so glad we agree. So would it be okay with you if I just did the best job I can on this outline and move forward with Chapter 1? Can you let me do just that tiny step? Will you help me?

Yes, I suppose so.

Woohoo—I win!

That was a really simple example. Often the freakout will give you a whole long list of reasons or excuses for why he's behaving a certain way.

When you do this exercise, make sure you address *everything* your freakout brings up when it's arguing with you. Every issue. Every complaint. Every word. Pay close attention, and you'll gain incredible clarity.

If you want to take this tool the extra mile, why not make those little guys work *for* you? They have direct access to your subconscious. And that part of you already knows the answers to any niggling writing problems you might come up against.

So ask the freakouts to research for you. Get them all together in your mind, even the ones you haven't met yet. Imagine you're having a writing meeting and you're the boss. Give them assignments. Just one at a time.

Hey, freakouts, I know you're sitting around with nothing to do at the moment, so how about you dig around and find the perfect subtitle for me?

OR

Okay, guys, we're all in this together. I know you're geniuses at digging things up out of my mind. So today I want you to figure out what Chapter 7 is all about. I'm wrapping up Chapter 6 today, so if you could bring me that insight by tomorrow morning, that'd be great.

Then set them loose. Give them a job to do, and they'll have less time to cause trouble.

I love giving my subconscious a job to do before I go to bed. Often I'll have the answer when I wake up. Or at the very least, I'll get an inkling while I'm in the shower or driving the kids to school.

It's magic! Get the freakouts on your side, keep them busy on little jobs that will help you out, and you might even get to like them. Plus it will be so much easier to talk them down when they misbehave.

It's all up to you. You have the power to create your reality with your thoughts and emotions—which is an awesome superpower and also an awesome responsibility.

It means you don't get to play the victim anymore. You don't get to say, "Poor me. I've got a terrible case of writer's block. I don't know if I'll ever finish this book." You now know that's just a freakout following a pattern. And you have the power to turn it around anytime you want. The only variables are how long it takes you to recognize the freakout and how long you decide to wait to get over it.

You want to be a prolific author?

You want best sellers flying off your keyboard at the speed of sound?

You want movie options and media appearances?

You want the dream career?

You can have it all. The Universe is saying yes! Get lightning fast at recognizing the freakouts and turning them into allies.

TOOL #2

LOVE LETTERS

Dear Reader,

You're worried, I know. You've got big dreams, and you're not sure how they'll ever come true.

Can I make it?

Am I good enough?

It's bad enough that your friends and family think you're crazy for even trying. But now you're beginning to question your own sanity. Wouldn't it be easier if you just gave up?

I see you. And I know what you're going through, because I *was* you! I've been in your shoes, and I know the agony of pursuing that creative dream when there's no evidence that you will ever succeed. I know how bad it stings to see rejection after rejection. It can stop you dead in your tracks.

But take heart, dear one. Because I've not only been where you are, I've also come out the other side. I've published my work. I've received public acclaim and awards, and the financial rewards that go along with them. I stopped many times. But I picked myself up again, dusted myself off, and kept going. And you can too!

If you're wondering whether it's worth all the struggle…

It absolutely is.

Keep going. And let this book be your guide. When you're tempted to give in, turn to these pages for hope and clarity.

You got this! I know you do.

Julie Anne Eason

IT'S TIME TO WRITE A LOVE LETTER TO YOUR HERO: THE READER OR PROTAGONIST.

Ooey-gooey love letters are the best way to remember your audience, purpose, and goal. Anytime you get off track or that brick wall is staring you in the face, go back and read your letter. Read it out loud. Get into the feelings behind the words.

This is no ordinary letter. It's a love letter. For nonfiction, it's laying out the great big WHY—the reason you're writing this book in the first place.

> Did you go through a bitter divorce and want to save others from the same fate?
>
> Were you abused as a child and want to help other survivors cope?
>
> Do you win blue ribbons at the state fair for baking your grandma's apple pie year after year and want to share that recipe with the world?
>
> Have you scaled your business from zero to $10 million in just a few years, and now it's time to give back?

Wherever you were is where your reader is now. So go back in time and remember how you felt going through that experience. Really feel it in your body. Pull up the emotions. It's okay to cry or laugh or feel any emotion that comes up.

Then picture one reader in your mind. And write directly to them. Tell them you know how hard they're struggling. Tell them you found a solution, and you promise to tell them all about it. Tell them they can trust you. They can depend on you. You won't let them down. You will finish this book for them.

Write as vividly as you can. If it's appropriate, make it painful. Make them squirm in their own discomfort. And then promise a way out.

Alternatively, you might make it funny. Drone on about how *tedious* it is to win blue ribbon after blue ribbon. Tell them this book is the answer to their apple pie dreams. And you're writing it because you just need some worthy competition. Make them laugh.

If you're writing fiction, write the letter to your protagonist. This will help you get into the character and let them speak to you about how frustrated they are, what they really want, and what they're willing to do to get it. Maybe even have a two-way conversation with them. Be as detailed as you can while still writing a letter (but not a whole notebook of procrasti-research).

Once you're done writing the letter, keep it handy. Anytime you feel lost or like you're staring at a brick wall and don't know what to do, it's time to get out of your head and into the heart of the story. And you do that by reminding yourself of your great big WHY.

So go back and read your letter. Get back into the emotions that prompted you to start your book in the first place.

It's magic.

Oh and one more thing… These love letters make an amazing preface, introduction, or other bit of front matter, especially for nonfiction books. (I usually title it "Dear Reader" as I did in this chapter.) You're grabbing your reader by the emotions and connecting with them *immediately*. They know you get them. They know you've been there and escaped. And they trust you have the solution right away. The letter erases any skepticism or resistance and just lets them read and absorb your words. Pretty sweet.

If love letters don't feel quite right, you could write a manifesto—a document that stakes a claim, plants a flag in the ground, and galvanizes a community or following. A manifesto helps the reader belong. They start with identification labels and phrases like…

> I am/We are…
>
> I/We believe…

It states what you (and they) stand for or are fighting against. It should be stirring and emotional and get the reader fired up!

The United States Constitution and Bill of Rights are manifestos of sorts. They state what we as a collective believe. The Constitution starts out by declaring who we are: "We the People of the United States…" Later it goes on to state what we believe and how we choose to behave as a country.

Another manifesto, the Declaration of Independence, very clearly states what we as Americans believe.

> We hold these truths to be self-evident, that all men are created equal, that they are endowed by their Creator with certain unalienable rights, that among these are Life, Liberty and the pursuit of Happiness.

Who doesn't want a piece of that?

If you're creating a movement or a community with a nonfiction book, it helps the reader understand the identity of the people who are part of the movement. They might not understand everything about what you're teaching, but they will be able to see themselves in your manifesto. That will help them realize they need to learn more. If they don't identify with your manifesto completely at first, they should by the end of the book.

One of my clients wrote a weight-loss book, and we knew that she was building a worldwide movement. Her people were different and strong and not afraid to do things differently. We galvanized them by giving them a name to call themselves (Code Red Rebels) and writing a manifesto to help them visualize what they believe. If they weren't Rebels at the beginning of the book, they sure were by the end! The manifesto helped them see what was possible and helped them *feel* what was possible when they joined the revolution and took on this new identity.

In a fiction book, you can use a similar tactic by helping the reader buy in to the premise of the book. Let them see themselves as part of the action. How many of us believe we really should have been educated at Hogwarts? Entire societies have been founded around fantasy worlds and fictional characters. Just spend an hour at Disneyland and you'll see the power of making fiction come to life using beliefs and identities.

Just remember this tool is not only for the reader. First and foremost, it's for you. It's there to motivate you and remind you of the reason you're doing all this in the first place. It's there to remind you of the responsibility you're shouldering on behalf of your future readers.

Sometimes I'll write a love letter to myself from Future Me, the one who is already finished with the project and knows how successful it becomes.

Future-pacing and visioneering are powerful tools. Even if this letter never makes it into your book, it's a powerful piece of writing. Read it often. Use it to help move you forward.

TOOL #3
MISSION STATEMENTS

It's time to pull out your Magic List again. You're going to use it to help you get through *any* tough writing task or life circumstance.

If your writing (or your life) is on the wrong feet, it's going to be tough to get through the day. Whether it's doing a complete chapter rewrite, negotiating an advance, or firing your agent, you want to face the day as your best self. And you already know who you are at your best because you wrote your list.

In order to *really* tap into your power as a human being, you'll use the words on your list as a kind of mantra for whatever you need in the moment. Damian calls it creating a mission statement, and it looks like this:

"I am _____, _____, and _____, so I can _____."

Fill in the first three blanks with words from your list that will help you accomplish the final blank, whatever it is. Here are some examples.

> I am productive, determined, and focused, so I can meet this deadline.
>
> I am creative, flowing, and free, so I can outline my new book.

I am strong, resolute, and sure, so I can negotiate my next advance.

I am abundant, resourceful, and friendly, so I can attract a new client at this networking meeting.

I know it might seem silly, but it works! When you consciously choose your emotional state to measure up to whatever challenge you have to deal with, life is so much easier. And it's not just for writing, by the way. You can choose your best-self state for any situation.

I am patient, kind, and even-tempered, so I can get through this holiday with my family.

I am bold, outspoken, and unafraid, so I can stand up for myself.

I am loving, playful, and joy-filled, so I can have a great day with my child.

You're setting your state based on how you want to feel for the next hour or the rest of the day. Take a minute or five to really anchor in the words you choose. Actually embody your best self for as long as you can.

You can change your mantra at any time. And if you feel yourself slipping out of alignment with your best self, just repeat it out loud or in your head. It's who you are. You don't have to fake it. It's not hard work to get there. It's your natural state when you are at your best.

It's okay if you're skeptical. Try it anyway. Keep repeating the mantra to yourself as you get through a small task like finishing a chapter or a tricky scene. Notice how much smoother the writing goes.

Does it go faster than normal?

Do you spend less time racking your brain for ideas?

Do the words flow easier?

The more you practice, the better it works!

TOOL #4

STARING FEAR IN THE FACE

When you get right down to it, the freakouts are just fear. That's all. Some fears are superficial, and others run to the very foundations of our identities. They are our core beliefs, formed when we were children, and they inform the decisions we make every day. Without our conscious permission, these beliefs are running the show.

The good news is that we have the power to change them.

Anytime we're triggered…

Anytime we feel a sickish feeling in our guts or a chest tightening when we read a negative review…

Anytime we feel anger rising up because someone did something to us, or someone is asking something of us…

Anytime something isn't fair…

We have the opportunity to stare fear in the face—really look at it—understand the false beliefs that support it, and vaporize it.

Really, it's true. It takes practice, but after a while you'll get really good at ferreting out the fear, staring it in the face, and banishing it from your life. And not just around your writing but with everything. After practicing this a while, your family won't bug you quite so much. You'll no longer dread conversations with your agent or publisher. You'll have the courage to ask for what you want. Best of all, the voices in your head will quiet down so you can get on with your work.

One more thing before you learn the process to overcome these fears.

Acknowledge that whatever you dig up, whatever false beliefs or unfounded fears you uncover, they are not the enemy. You are not the enemy. There is no enemy! Your subconscious is first and foremost concerned with your safety and survival. Its primary job is to preserve the status quo. Because right now you're alive. You're breathing. And that's all that matters. And any beliefs it can muster to keep you stuck in place are tools it will use to make sure that happens.

Be gentle with yourself. But when it comes to having conversations with your fear, the gloves come off. You've been allowing the freakouts to run the show, but now you're taking charge. Sometimes the only way to deal with the fear is to stare it down and command it to leave. (You are such a badass!)

Okay, here's how you vaporize your fears.

STEP 1: NOTICE THE CHARGE.

Your freakout uses a charge or a trigger like a psychic taser gun every time you step out of line or look like you might just be getting somewhere. Subconscious beliefs and fear show up in the physical body as charges.

These vary from person to person. For some, it's a sick feeling in the belly. Others get an instant headache or their heart space starts to ache. All it takes is one zap from a trigger to set start the self-conditioning recorded loop playing in your head.

Pay attention to your body and you'll soon pick up on your own pattern. When you notice a charge, get quiet and ask yourself, *What's really going on here?*

Sometimes there is no charge, but you're not getting anywhere. You're doing the work but not making any noticeable forward progress. You just feel stuck in spite of doing everything you know you're supposed to do. It's possible you actually *are* making progress, but you just can't see it. But it's equally possible that something deep down is blocking your efforts. Something you believe has its foot firmly on the brake. So again ask, *What's really going on here?*

When you start uncovering beliefs and staring down fears, it can be tempting to get down on yourself.

How could I be so stupid?

This belief comes straight from my parents. It's not me!

How many more books could I have written in all the time I've been stuck?

It doesn't matter how much time you've spent under the spell of these beliefs and fears. It only matters that you are now making a different choice, and you know how to get unstuck anytime you want. So even though you're about to have a down-and-dirty fight with yourself, be kind. You've been doing the best you can.

STEP 2: LET THE CHARGE SPEAK.

Write down everything it says to you *word-for-word*. Don't just play out the conversation in your head. You are about to uncover a fear based on a belief you formed early in your life. This is a core part of you that you've probably spent decades ignoring or burying deep down inside you. Addictions have been built to help keep that belief buried. You've developed coping mechanisms and numbing agents like food, drink, shopping, sleeping, maybe even reading too much to keep you from feeling the charge and actually confronting it.

When you stop ignoring it and stare it in the face, it's going to defend itself. Its very life depends on you believing whatever it says. It will produce evidence and put on a great show. But you must understand…THE CHARGE LIES. Always. Otherwise it wouldn't be standing between you and what you want. It wouldn't be helping you procrastinate. It wouldn't be whispering hurtful things in your ear.

You've come this far—don't be afraid to face your own beliefs. They will try to shame you. They will try to prove they're right and you're wrong with very reasonable evidence. Remember, these are only thoughts. They are only beliefs. You are allowed to change your mind (and your heart) anytime you want. It doesn't make you an idiot just because you believed "Life isn't fair" or "I'll never make money as a writer" for the past 47 years.

STEP 3: REFUTE EVERY STATEMENT WITH THE TRUTH UNTIL IT GIVES IN AND THE CHARGE GOES AWAY.

The Truth (with a capital T) is your new belief. The thing you know is *actually TRUE* rather than what you once believed to be true.

You're playing the prosecuting attorney here, and your best strategy is to get the witness to provide proof that what they're saying is true. Keep asking questions to pull out everything that fear has in its back pocket, *everything* it's been using to keep you stuck or afraid, including the payoffs you get for continuing to believe it.

Answer every single idea it brings up with the capital-T Truth. You can even make a game out of it and pretend you're a four-year-old who wants capital-A Answers. A four-year-old Never. Gives. Up.

Yeah, but WHYYYYY? Why can't we get ice cream?

Why do we have to go to the bank first? Then we can get ice cream?

Why not? Why why why?

Wear the argument down. You've got all day. Everything it can come up with, every lie and false belief. You've got the Truth.

STEP 4: REINFORCE YOUR NEW TRUE BELIEF.

You can make up a mantra for yourself. Just a few words that you repeat over and over to yourself to anchor in the Truth. You can even use words from your list to help. The more you repeat the Truth, the more embedded it will become in your psyche. The old belief might try to come back, it might even disguise itself as something else, but you will recognize it and have the Truth on your side.

Once you've been integrating your new belief for a while, experiment a little. Repeat a behavior or talk to someone who used to trigger you and see if the same charge appears. Hopefully it will be gone completely. But if it's still there, it should be greatly diminished. If for some reason it's not, then you haven't completely dissolved the belief. Or others have sprung up in its place. Don't worry, you haven't failed—you just have more work to do.

When you first start using this process, you might find you need to have more than one conversation with the freakouts. They might go away and come back with more evidence. They might bring reinforcements. That's okay.

One by one, dissolve the beliefs and replace them with the Truth. After a while, it gets easier, and you can blast through a belief in just a few minutes with no drama or tears…until eventually there's little or nothing left to unearth. You've completely transformed from caterpillar to butterfly. You're a completely different person living an abundant, amazing, creative life on your terms. The full transformation can take months or years. Let it. Take your time. You're doing great!

Here's an example of this process in action. You're an individual with your own past experiences that shaped who you are and what you believe. However, many core beliefs about writing and creativity and abundance have remarkably similar roots. Just follow the flow of the conversation and then replicate it with your own freakouts anytime you feel a charge or trigger.

SAMPLE CONVERSATION

Situation: Your best friend sends you an ad for a writing contest and encourages you to enter.

1.   Notice the charge.

You read the ad and click Learn More to get the full scoop. From the description, you think, *Wow, this is actually perfect for me.*

It's right up my alley. And there's some nice prize money too. And a meeting with a publisher? I should totally do this.

Then BAM! Within seconds, you feel your chest tighten, and right on cue the freakouts show up with all the reasons you can't enter.

Yeah, but the deadline is in two weeks. I couldn't possibly finish my manuscript in time. Besides, this project isn't really that good. I mean, it's okay…but it's not a contest winner. I wouldn't have a chance, so why rush to submit and put all that stress on myself?

This is your cue to ask, "What's really going on here?"

2. Let the freakout speak (knowing that everything he says is a lie). Write down everything he has to say.

Well, you know your writing is just a hobby, right? I mean, you're never going to make a living at it. You're not that good. Mrs. Brown told you as much in fifth grade. What was it she said? Your writing "showed no imagination." That was it.

So are you really going to work your butt off to submit something to a contest? Imagine the humiliation! There's no chance you're going to win. You'll just be setting yourself up for heartbreak and a month of crying into a tub of ice cream.

You don't want to ruin your shot at getting a publisher someday, do you? What if they read your manuscript and it's terrible? Like, the worst thing they've ever read. They'll ban you forever. They'll tell all their friends to never publish anything you send them.

Besides, you're really busy at work. You'd have to stay up late to finish by the deadline, and you can't afford to lose your job. Stop being a dreamer like Uncle Arthur and come back down to reality. Contests are for professionals, not for you.

3.   Refute the freakout with the Truth, line by line.

First take a deep breath and get a little (or a lot) pissed off at what your freakout is saying to you. Pull on your Power Pants and let 'er rip!

> *You know your writing is just a hobby, right? I mean, you're never going to make a living from it.*

Okay, first of all, is that really true? Just because I'm not making money at it right now doesn't mean it's a hobby. I take my work seriously. And I have dreams of turning it into a full-time thing. I'm *never* going to make a living at it? Really? WATCH ME!

> *You're not that good. Mrs. Brown told you as much in fifth grade. What was it she said? Your writing "showed no imagination." That was it.*

Fifth grade? That's all you got? Mrs. Brown was a horrible teacher and had no idea what she was talking about. And that was DECADES ago. I am not the same person. I am not a child. I've practiced my craft. And I continue to work on it consistently.

And what does "that good" even mean anyway? What's your basis for comparison? Every writer is always learning. I get better all the time. This is a bullshit argument. What's really going on here?

> *So you're really going to work your butt off to submit something to a contest? Imagine the humiliation! There's no chance you're going to win. You'll just be setting yourself up for heartbreak and a month of crying into a tub of ice cream.*

Is that actually true? Do you know for sure that I won't win? What if I do? What if there's celebration and joy? Humiliation is a feeling, and I know how to control my feelings. That means any potentially humiliating situation can be reframed in my mind as a learning experience and nothing more.

And "heartbreak" is a tad overdramatic, don't you think? Not winning a contest is hardly on the same level as losing the love of my life. I can be happy if I win and sad if I don't win without being overly attached. It's just one contest. And my ice cream habits are none of your business! What's *really* going on here?

> *You don't want to ruin your shot at getting a publisher someday, do you? What if they read your manuscript and it's terrible? Like, the worst thing they've ever read. They'll ban you forever. They'll tell all their friends to never publish anything you send them.*

Okay, for real? You think publishers have time to sit around and ban random writers they *might* come across someday. That's RIDICULOUS! Publishers have to wade through hundreds if not thousands of manuscripts a month. They have to meet with agents to find the ones with the best shot at making a profit.

And honestly, even IF what you're saying were true (which it's not), there are SO MANY WAYS to publish a book these days. Even IF there were some magical Do Not Publish Ever list somewhere (which there's not), I'm not going to let that stop me. There are a million books published each year, and only a handful come from traditional publishers. My success depends on me, not anyone else. I don't believe this one either. What else ya got?

> *Besides, you're really busy at work. You'd have to stay up late to finish by the deadline, and you can't afford to lose your job. Stop being a dreamer like Uncle Arthur and come back down to reality. Contests are for professionals, not for you.*

Aha! There it is—my mother's voice. She always said, "Don't be like Arthur. He's such a dreamer. He'll never amount to anything in his life." This is the real reason you don't want me to enter that contest. Because I might actually win. And I might be encouraged by the prize money. I might even start entertaining notions of quitting my day job and writing full-time. Then what? I might become a loser like Mom's brother? I might struggle for money like he did? She is so proud of my career right now. If she knew I was writing at night and entering contests, it would crush her.

Is THAT what's really going on here? Because that's a load of crap!

I am a grown-ass adult and am in control of my own life. My mother has no say in whether I'm a lawyer or a writer. And by the way, not for nothing, I am NOT Uncle Arthur. I am ME. Just because I might quit my job to write full-time does not mean I'll fail. It does not mean I'll squander all my money traveling to write in exotic places.

And what's so wrong with that anyway? Mom thinks her brother is a loser, but he's actually pretty cool. Maybe the truth is that Mom's jealous of the fact that he gets to do whatever he wants. He gets to travel and have fun, and people pay him for it. Maybe he doesn't make as much as she does, but he's free. So let's not compare me to him, m'kay? Because that's crap and we both know it.

And by the way, contests are NOT for professionals. They are for amateurs who want to test their mettle and get constructive feedback. They are for people who want to gain the attention of publishers. Especially this one—it says so right on the website! So don't give me this crap about "I'm not good enough to enter this contest." I am and I will. And whatever happens will not crush me or humiliate me or cause Mom to disown me.

Do you have anything else to say, Freakout? Huh? Lay it on me!

[*Crickets.*]

This is your last chance to put up a fight. Nothing? Okay! I'm doing it. I'm entering that contest right now, and then I'm working on my manuscript every spare moment until the deadline. And you know what? I do have a shot at winning! Because I am amazing at what I do.

4. REINFORCE YOUR NEW TRUE BELIEF. USE YOUR MAGIC LIST TO HELP YOU.

I am creative, focused, and efficient...so I can finalize this book and get it off to the contest.

I am determined, patient, and hopeful...so I can keep my dreams of full-time writing alive.

I write better and better all the time. My passion shows through my work, and no matter what happens with this opportunity, there will always be more of them.

Did you notice that the freakout's excuses started off flimsy and ridiculous and then got more serious as I dug deeper? The more times you ask...

"What's really going on here?"

"Is that actually TRUE?"

"What else ya got?"

…the more likely you'll land on the true issue that's holding you back, the root cause of your resistance.

You'll know it when you see it. That's why it's so important to write this conversation out on paper. Things that seem big and scary in your head tend to be nothing at all when written out and viewed objectively.

Your freakouts will tell you to wait, that you're not good enough, it's too risky, people will gossip about you, there's no way you'll succeed—so you'd better play it safe. Every negative scenario is made up. But each one is cleverly dressed up in facts based on *your past experiences*.

It's a fact from your past that Mrs. Brown said your writing lacked imagination, and those words hurt you deeply.

It's a fact from your past that your mom thinks her brother is a loser.

It's a fact from your past that she's happy you have a secure job and proud of your accomplishments.

But it's *conjecture* that she will be devastated and disown you if you choose to become a full-time writer.

Look for the false lines of logic. A + B = C only works with numbers, not emotions.

In middle school, I was the top student in everything. I was the smartest at math, history, and especially English. So when I lost the all-school spelling bee on the very first word, it was humiliating. Everyone laughed at me. And I spent the next 10 years thinking that meant I couldn't spell. Which in turn meant I was a terrible writer.

But it meant no such thing. It was just a moment in time. It was just bad luck. I was 10 years old, for crying out loud! But I beat myself up for it, and I still remember that moment to this day. (*Recipe.* How could I miss such a simple word?)

Once you shine a light of Truth on the false logic, your subconscious will loosen its grip. It will take its foot off the brake and actually start to help you achieve your conscious desires. But you have to clear *every* argument it has, no matter how ridiculous or painful they are. You have to stare the fear in the face and let it know who's boss.

Fear isn't real. We make it up. And we can unmake it too.

Danger is real; fear is a choice.

The example above was a pretty benign conversation with a freakout. The conversations can get much more heated and emotional. They can dredge up long-buried and forgotten feelings. They can rip off scar tissue over a wound you thought you had healed decades ago so that the pain is fresh once again.

Don't let that scare you. Staring fear in the face is essential if you want to truly move past your freakouts, blocks, and resistance.

And chances are that anything that painful is affecting far more than your writing. It's affecting your entire life. The healing is worth it.

> Important Note: Sometimes you'll uncover things that qualify as genuine trauma. If that happens, please don't hesitate to get professional help to process and heal it. We bury things for a good reason. Sometimes we need help handling what we dredge up!

Humans have a unique ability to take any experience and spin it into stories that provide meaning. And from those stories, we create rules for how we should live our lives going forward.

Daddy praised you once for being such a pretty princess.

Right—got it! I'm wearing floral dresses for the rest of my life. No tattoos and leather for me. Uh-uh, no matter how bad I want it! Gotta follow the rules. I'm a pretty princess, not a badass.

We also invent fear.

If I'm not a pretty princess when I visit Dad, he will be disappointed in me. So I will keep one dress in my closet, just for holiday visits.

Do you see how silly that is?

There's no wrong way to do this. As long as you're getting to the root of the fear that's fueling your freakout, you're doing it right. The process can take as much time as it needs. And you will get faster the more often you do it.

It helps me to picture the freakout shrinking down from the terrifying, bossy monster who thinks he's in charge to a cute little guy with a gift.

The gift is certainty and peace.

You are the boss of you. Even if you forgot for a little while.

TOOL #5
CHANGE YOUR STATE

I was heartbroken, sobbing, waiting by the telephone, praying it would ring any second.

"Okay, in three seconds, he's going to call…"

[3, 2, 1…nothing]

"Okay, okay…five seconds…"

[nothing]

"Please, God, please let him call…"

If you don't remember a time when people waited by the phone, we did it because the phone was literally (get this) attached to the wall. And there was only one per household, unless you were extremely lucky and your mom got tired of answering your calls. That meant one phone number for everyone living in the same house. (Imagine!)

Regardless of your personal phone status, if you've ever been a teenager in love, you know what I'm talking about. Those painful hours when you're just *sure* they're out with someone else, making jokes about you and mocking your pain. Your chest is tight. Your eyes are sore from crying. You're spinning out in your brain, imagining all sorts of terrible scenarios.

Maybe he's been in a horrible accident and he can't call because he's in the hospital in a coma! Relationship freakouts send your brain into all sorts of crazy places.

Then you see him at school on Monday morning. Acting like nothing happened. How *dare* he smile at you and ask, "How's it going?" Doesn't he know how much you suffered over the weekend? Doesn't he *care*?!

Best not let him see you're upset. "Oh, I'm good. Yeah, fine. I, uh, missed you this weekend."

You wait for his shifty excuses. But he just casually mentions that he was fishing with his family out in the woods and got home late last night. "Sorry, no cell service at the lake. Want to hit the arcade after school?"

And just like that, everything is okay again. You realize that you spent an entire weekend worrying about absolutely nothing. You created the entire scenario *in your mind* and got yourself into an *agitated state* for no reason.

We do this to ourselves all the time. We create situations and scenarios in our brains and then act them out as if they were real. Reality is 100% dependent on our self-created state of mind.

Our state can set us on edge, make us paranoid, or give us a full-on anxiety attack. Our state can also set us at ease, make us grateful and proud, and give us new creative ideas. We buy in to the story our state is spinning so completely that it affects our physiology. We *feel* hyped up or nervous. We *experience* shortness of breath or chest pains, even when there's no physical reason for it. That's how powerful our brains are.

The beautiful thing is that we have the power to control our state at will…if we choose to. You might not realize it, but anytime you're spinning out with wild scenarios like…

> *This screenplay is crap, no agent is going to be interested.*
>
> *My mother was right—I should have been a doctor.*
>
> *I must be crazy thinking this book is any good.*

...you have the power to turn it around. You can experience the exact opposite emotion if you choose to.

Changing your state is surprisingly easy, once you're aware that you have the ability to do it. It can be as simple as spending a few minutes on a mindful breathing exercise, going for a run, turning on your favorite song and dancing out the bad juju, or lighting a candle and centering yourself with some positive affirmations.

Whatever tool you use, taming the freakouts is all about changing your state. Getting yourself into the physical and emotional state you need to be in to do the work in front of you. That can be tricky if you aren't aware of the different states you go through during the day. Do any of these sound familiar?

- The scrolling-through-social-media state
- The distracted-by-a-day-job state
- The busy-busy-busy-till-you-drop-into-bed state
- The languorous, floaty, I-don't-really-wanna state
- The gotta-put-the-family-first state
- The gotta-cook-dinner-then-do-dishes-then-give-the-kids-a-bath-and-tuck-them-in state
- The voices-in-my-head state
- The I-must-be-crazy-thinking-I-can-be-a-real-writer state

Exhausted yet? Here's how to become the boss of your energetic state.

1. Become aware of your state.
2. Physically change it.

BECOME AWARE OF YOUR STATE.

Consider setting a reminder on your phone and doing a check-in on your mental and physical states every few hours.

What's running through your mind?

How do you feel physically?

What's your energy doing?

If you've been sitting for a long time and your energy is stagnant, it's probably time to shake things out and get back to a more active and alert state.

If you've been shuttling kids all over town and running errands in between soccer and ballet, maybe it's time for a more calming state. Become present with your activities instead of letting your mind race a million miles an hour about everything you need to do.

Don't judge where you are—just notice and decide whether you want to stay there or shift to something better.

PHYSICALLY CHANGE YOUR STATE.

That means changing your blood-oxygen level and adjusting the hormones/neurotransmitters currently flooding your system. If you're stressed out, you're probably not breathing deeply, which means you're depriving yourself of oxygen. And you've got all kinds of nasty chemicals like cortisol and adrenaline running through your system making you feel the way you do.

Just breathing in slowly for as little as one minute will dramatically alter your state. Slow, deep breathing—especially longer exhales—activates your vagus nerve. That's a nerve that starts in your head and winds all throughout your body. It is the main component of your parasympathetic nervous system. (That's the parts of you that happen automatically, without you even thinking about it.) The vagus nerve is responsible for loads of critical functions in your body including your mood, immune response, digestion, and heart rate.

All you have to do to change your state and silence a freakout's voice in your head is to alter your breathing for a few minutes. It's easy, it works, and it's free! You can do it anytime you're feeling out of sorts.

Here's a simple breathing exercise you can try anytime, anywhere.

1. Breathe in deeply through your nose for a count of 4. Allow your diaphragm and lungs to fill up. Your belly should get bigger. Don't suck it in like you're trying to fit into tight jeans.

2. Exhale through your mouth slooowly for 6 or 8 counts.

3. Repeat this 5 or 10 times.

How do you feel? Are the voices quieter? Hopefully they're gone and you can focus on the work in front of you. If not, keep doing the breath work.

I like to boost the simple breathing with a little visualization exercise, especially if the brain clutter is really getting in my way. All those little nagging questions and negative statements, like…

Who am I to write a book? Who do I think I am?

Why am I doing this? This is so stupid.

Oh my gosh, what do I think I'm doing?

No one's going to buy this script.

No one's going to read this book.

No one's going to find this blog post or care about it.

No one's going to comment on my social media.

All that noise—it's in your head. You're making it up. And the freakouts love it!

When you allow those thoughts into your brain and then into your body, they infect you, and the infection will stop you.

It will stop your writing.

It will stop you getting your message out into the world.

It will keep you small, and it will keep you quiet.

That's not what you want. Your voice needs to be heard. Your message needs to be heard. Your book needs to be written. We need you to keep writing.

So how do you do that? How do you literally turn down the noise in your head so that you can get back to writing?

I call this exercise Turn Down The Noise. (I know—creative, right?) You're gonna get uncomfortable first, and then you're going to get more comfortable, okay? Read through this entire description, then try it out for yourself.

The first thing you're gonna do is tune in and feel that noise.

1. Close your eyes and take a few deep breaths. You're just centering yourself and getting into your body and your mind. Breathe in through your nose, out through your mouth. Pay attention to your breath for 3 cycles.

2. Now visualize those questions that are in your brain right now.

Who am I to do this?

Why am I doing this?

Who do I think I am?

Whatever questions are making you feel less than your best, bring them to mind. Let them speak. Go ahead. It's all right.

3. If you start shaking or you start crying, that's okay. That's good. Allow yourself to feel the noise and locate where it is in your body.

How does this make my heart feel?

How does it make my stomach feel?

How about my head? Is it in a vise?

Are my muscles tight?

Am I scared?

How do those voices in my head make me feel in my body?

Are they trying to tell me something? What is it?

Now, do you *want* to feel that? Do you like that feeling? Or do you want to get rid of it? (I'm going to assume you want to get rid of it.)

Let's evaporate and release these feelings so you can get back to writing. Let's turn down the noise. You may not get rid of it completely. And you may have to come back and do this a few times. But you can do it anytime you want, as often as you want. This is your tool, and you get to use it to control how you're feeling.

1. Take another deep breath, fully aware of all those negatives in your body right now.

2. Picture a black dial in front of you. It's attached to a pressure valve. And it goes all the way up to 11. What level is your noise right now? How intense is the anxiety or desire to procrastinate? Is it a 4? Is it an 8? Or is it all the way up to 11? Can you picture it? Good.

3. Instead of procrasti-whatevering right now, you're going to just feel the pain, fear, or whatever emotions are coming up for you. Acknowledge them. Thank them for keeping you safe, but tell them that they are no longer required. Their service is done. You don't need them anymore.

4. Reach your hand out and physically turn that imaginary dial down a few notches. As you do, you're going to quiet the noise in your head and release the tension in your body, the same way you would quiet a crying child.

5. Take a deep breath in (count to 4), mentally turn that dial down, and at the same time exhale a long Shhhhhhhhhhhhhhh…(to the count of 6 or 8).

   Shhhhhhhhhhhhh. It's okay. Everything is good.

6. Repeat this cycle (inhale for 4 and exhale shhhhhh for 6 or 8) at least 5 times. Every time you exhale, release more of the pressure. Dissolve the fear. Imagine it leaving your body.

You should feel relaxed yet energized. And whatever was bothering or distracting you should be fully released. If those noises are still in your head or you still feel a little bit of a negative charge in your body, do it again. Take a deep breath, reach out, and turn that dial down. Don't stuff the feeling down into your body. Pull it up and out of you with your breath.

Shhhhhhhhhhhh. It's okay. You can write for a while. Nothing will fall apart if you do.

That crying child you're comforting is yourself, the part of you that's freaking out. You're telling yourself that it's okay to feel those negative feelings. It's okay to have self-doubt. It's okay. It's also okay to let them go. And it's okay to keep writing even if the feelings are still there.

The freakouts want you to stop, but you won't. You will keep going. You will get back to your writing and that noise in your head will go away, even if it's just for a little while.

It's okay. Everything's fine. You're safe. And you're doing your work.

One more time—reach out and turn the dial down.

Shhhhhhhhhhhh. It's okay.

Reach out and turn the dial down. Do this as many times as you need to until you feel confident, then get yourself back to work. Okay?

You got this. I know you do.

EXTRA CREDIT: TURN THE VOLUME UP

Want to really ramp up the power? After you've released the negative charge and turned the volume down to 0 (or near enough), imagine a different dial. This one is connected to a giant receiver. It can look fancy—maybe a golden color or green or whatever makes you happy. Mine sparkles like a sea of diamonds in the sunlight.

When you feel like the noise and negative feelings have pretty much gone, imagine this new dial is set to low, like maybe a 1 or even a 0 if you aren't feeling motivated at all yet. You can ask this receiver to pick up *any channel you desire*. Ask it for anything you want.

> If you need to write a steamy sex scene and you're not sure how, imagine yourself writing it beautifully.
>
> If you need to distill a complicated medical procedure down to the level that a first-year medical student could understand, imagine yourself figuring out a brilliant new framework.
>
> Need to write a book for a client? Channel their ideas and their voice right through this connection.

Literally whatever you need for motivation or understanding or creativity is available to you with that glittering dial.

Once you have the image in your head, return to your breathing. Inhale for 4 counts, exhale for 6 or 8. And in your mind's eye, imagine turning the dial UP during your exhalation. You're *increasing* the intensity this time instead of turning it down.

Whatever you're asking for is energy. And every time you turn the dial up, you're building the potential energy inside yourself. Feel the excitement rising in your body. Let it fill you up completely.

Turn that sucker ALL the way up, until your body is buzzing with creativity!

Until the thought of waiting one more second to write that next chapter is almost painful.

Like you *have to* write. You *can't wait* another instant.

Then open your eyes and write.

Let the energy you just generated sustain you. Let it be the magic that flows through you and out your fingertips. Let it be a river that just flows effortlessly. Instead of *thinking* about what to write, just allow the words to come.

You're tapping into the quantum field of infinite possibilities and ultimate creativity. If you practice this regularly, you'll soon find yourself able to stay tuned in for longer and longer periods of time. And you'll probably figure out that you can use this same breathing and visualization technique for other areas of your life.

> Want more confidence so you can ask that person you like out on a date? Turn up the volume on your confidence.
>
> Want to ace an exam? Turn up the volume on your memory and focus.
>
> Want to push that baby out of you? You can't get much more intense than that. (Yeah, there's a reason childbirth professionals teach breath work.)

You have a direct line to the Universe, and you can ask for anything you want. But the Universe doesn't speak English or Chinese or Arabic. It speaks energy and frequency. It speaks emotions and feelings. So using your breath combined with visualizations sends out a clear signal and allows an open channel for your incoming genius.

Try it. I think you'll love it.

IT'S ALL UP TO YOU NOW

The *audience* for this book is writers—all kinds of writers, but specifically book authors.

The *purpose* is to move them from a stuck state of overwhelm, confusion, and self-doubt to a place where the writing flows and the freakouts don't bother them anymore.

The *goal* for me as the author is to publish, because that's what I was put on this earth to do.

I dedicated this book to myself because it's the book I wish I'd had over 30 years ago. If I had, maybe my life would be completely different. Maybe I'd have become a teenage novelist. Or maybe I'd be on a worldwide speaking tour promoting my fifteenth book by now.

But here's the thing—I believe everything happens for a reason. Divine timing is real. And until we learn the lessons we're meant to learn, we are doomed to repeat the same mistakes and fall into the same traps.

Writing can be hard...or it can be easy. It's your choice.

I know that sounds flippant or dismissive, but it's true. You create your reality, based on your deeply embedded beliefs. You probably didn't consciously choose those beliefs; you adopted them when you were a child, in reaction to things that happened to you.

Writers don't make money.

You should get a real job.

Nobody reads books these days.

Only the lucky ones rise to the top.

You don't have the talent.

Whatever it is the freakouts whisper to you, they're lies. They're the beliefs you hold about yourself. And you have the power to change them.

I believe the Universe always says YES, no matter what statement you put before it.

Writing books is hard. (Yes, that's true!)

Writing books is easy. (Yes, that's true!)

I don't know what I'm doing. (Yes! You don't know what you're doing, ya poor bastard.)

I don't know what I'm doing, but I'm learning, and this book is going to be amazing. (Yes! You don't know what you're doing, but you're learning and this book is going to be amazing. You're so lucky!)

Whatever you state as fact, the Universe will agree with you.

Therefore, whatever you believe is true IS true.

This is the source of the freakouts' power over you.

The amount of time it takes to write a book and how easy or hard the process is for you—ultimately it's all within your control.

A WORD OF CAUTION

I love reading self-development and spirituality books. And for a long time, the more I read, the more I thought was wrong with me. I would google symptoms for the common cold and decide I MUST have leprosy, and surely my left leg is going to drop off any minute now.

But sometimes (most of the time), there's nothing wrong with me. I'm not sabotaging myself because I feel unworthy to write because of something my father did 40 years ago. Sometimes I just need to get better at managing my time. Sometimes I just need to get over myself and *do the damn work*.

It's tempting to go down the path of analyzing...

WHY OH WHY am I not able to write?

WHY can't I get this book out to my editor?

WHY aren't my tiny attempts at marketing bringing in thousands of followers?

Woe is me!

Introspection is valuable, but it can be its own kind of trap. Sometimes I'm not doing it because I'm just *not doing it*. But if I decide I'm going to do it, then I will.

Don't overanalyze yourself to pieces. Give yourself a freakin' break. If writing an hour a day is too much for your schedule, cut it in half. If reaching out to five podcasts a week is taking too long, just do one. Small progress begets big progress. It all adds up.

Maybe you're not stuck at all. Maybe it's just *thinking* you're stuck that's stopping you. You'll know when this is the case because once you start doing the work, everything will begin to flow.

I've seen these freakouts so many times that now I recognize them almost instantly. They play out in exactly the same way for me, for my colleagues, and for my clients. The fears may manifest differently in each author, but I can see when an obstacle is really fear. And based on when in the writing or publishing process it's happening, I can tell which freakout is running the show and how to deal with it. And now you can too.

You have two options.

1. You can choose to let the freakouts control you. You can spin out in your excuses and life circumstances forever. You can let your dreams of being an author remain just dreams. There's a payoff for that—only you know what it is.

2. Or you can choose to deal with the fear behind the freakout. There's a payoff for that too.

One of my clients talks about "riding with the fear." She knows that she pushes her limits all the time and that fear is just part of the equation. So she just accepts that it's always going to be there. But she puts it in the back seat. She doesn't let fear drive her. It's along for the ride, but she refuses to allow it to control any of her decisions.

I have other clients who choose to release the fear, to cut it out and not allow it to return. Of course, it always does—that's just part of being human. But every time they recognize it, they banish it from their lives. And the more they do it, the faster they get at recognizing it and the easier it is to release. Which means it has less of an effect, causes less of a maelstrom, and becomes just an annoying sprinkle of rain that soon passes.

Choosing to write is an act of courage. We live in a digital age of temporary thoughts.

Someone took offense at your blog post? You can take it down if you want to.

You found a typo or misquoted fact in your e-book? You can change it in a matter of minutes, and likely no one will be the wiser.

You can continually correct and change your stance on social media.

But a book is permanent. Your words are printed on physical sheets of paper. You can't take them back—and that's scary.

You know what's even scarier? The fact that *anyone* can publish *anything* in book form. There are no gatekeepers to the publishing world anymore. No one is evaluating every manuscript and deciding whether it's worthy to be put out into the world.

As messed up as that model of traditional publishing was, it did provide some layer of protection. If you were picked up by an agent or publisher, that meant at least someone who knew what they were doing thought your ideas were worthy of becoming a book. It gave you some sense of confidence, which I imagine would make the freakouts easier to deal with.

Modern publishing is a double-edged sword. If you want to be an author, you can be. Period. The playing field has been leveled, the barriers to entry removed.

But you have to provide your own confidence. You have to deem yourself worthy. You have to believe that your ideas are meaningful and that your writing will find its audience.

So many writers never get there. And 97% of books never get finished.

But as for you…

You now recognize the early signs of freaking out.

You know where to look for the fear and what to do about it.

You even have sneaky ways of making the freakouts work for you.

You will write and publish amazing books that inspire, educate, entertain, and sell.

And so will I.

It's time for me to put this book to bed. It will go to my beta readers next, and then it's off to the editor. (I wonder if that sentence will make the cut.) I still have Freakouts #4 and #5 to go on this one, but I know what to do. And if you're reading these words, it means I didn't let those little buggers stop me.

And if I can do it, so can you.

I believe in you!

Julie Anne Eason

ONE MORE THING...

As I was putting this book to bed, it asked me for a glass of water and just one more story.

In other words, it wasn't done yet. It had a little more to say.

And I realized something...

My book has a consciousness. It's a living, breathing thing. It came from the formless void into this world as a solid creation through me. And it has a job to do.

It never occurred to me to ask my book what its mission is.

It never occurred to me to ask it what it wanted to say.

It never occurred to me that my book could be my very best resource for writing itself.

This entire book has been all about you. Giving form and feeling and motive to the crazy-making thoughts in your head. Why? So you can talk to them, reason with them, get them to take their feet off the brake and help you move forward. So *you* can be the boss of your book, not the freakouts.

But your book is really the boss. It knows what it needs to be. It understands things you have yet to realize. And if you can allow yourself to be a conduit for your book to come into being, the resistance disappears. Writing no longer feels like a chore that you don't really have time for. Instead, it can become the best part of your day, just hanging out with a dear friend and listening to what they have to say.

When you hit a particularly sticky section, you have two choices.

1. You can be the boss and wrestle with the words for hours or days or months.

2. You can let the book be the boss. Ask the book for the solution—it knows.

And before you say it, yes I know this sounds a little silly. But what's wrong with that? Allowing your book to have a mind of its own—to challenge you, to make you rework your assumptions—that's magic! That's cocreating with the Universe, or God, or Source, or whatever you believe is bigger than you.

I think this is what some people call a muse. And I also think every book is its *own* muse. It is unique and has its own qualities and characteristics.

Your first book might be a crotchety old man railing against the complexities of technology. Your next one might be a little girl chasing butterflies through the tall grass of your book's pages. Is there danger lurking in the grass? Or a surprise? Your book knows.

I believe there is value in allowing your book to become what it was meant to become, so it can do what it came here to do. And I don't know any better way to find out what your book really is than to help it create its own Magic List! (You didn't see that coming, did you, Damian?)

I'd never thought to create a list for a book until this very moment. So play along with me, okay? Here's what *The 5 Author Freakouts* is at its best...

It is hopeful.

It is inspiring.

It is light.

It is courageous.

It is "out there."

It is true.

It is encouraging.

It is funny.

It is loving.

It is creative.

It is cheerful.

It is energetic.

It is fun.

It is playful.

It is insightful.

It is thought-provoking.

It is lively.

It is smiling.

It is daring.

It is brave.

It is challenging.

It is questioning.

It is unusual.

It is simple.

It is experimental.

It is tricky.

It is happy.

It is magic.

Well, that's a great start anyway. Sometimes it takes a while to find all 60 adjectives.

It's interesting to note how similar this list is to my own. But I don't think that's always the case, especially if you're writing fiction. I think the bigger the difference between who you are and what your book is, the more important it is to create a separate Magic List for your book. Let it become a living, breathing thing.

Try it. And let me know what comes from it.

This is all a grand experiment, this Universe of ours. And we have the honor, responsibility, and privilege to write it all down.

Go write. I can't wait to read your book!

YOU CAN HELP OTHER WRITERS BEAT THE FREAKOUTS

The world needs more voices, more books, more stories and that means we need more published authors. 97% of books that are started never get finished and that breaks my heart.

Now that you know how to recognize and deal with these guys, you can help spread the word.

Share this book with your friends, writing groups, editors, publishers, and teachers.

And while you're at it, please leave a review on Amazon, Goodreads, or your favorite review sites.

Together we can write our way to a better world!

ACKNOWLEDGEMENTS

This book has been a long time coming. As I coached client after client through their freakouts, I started to see the patterns. And when my team was able to recognize and coach me through them, that's when I knew the freakouts needed their own book.

I have to thank my family for continually supporting me in all kinds of ways while I write and write and write some more. You're all the best friends a person could have in this life.

Erin Neuhardt, thank you for kicking me through Freakout #1 and making me finally write this book.

Francis Duvall, your illustrations made my words come alive. Thank you!

Kevin LeBlanc, thank you for being part of my life and my business. Your masterful handling of the publishing details made this book come alive.

Julie Willson, as always, thank you for being an incredible editor and friend. You deserve a medal of honor for how many author freakouts you've endured.

Laura Howard, thank you for making this book so beautiful inside and out.

Damian Boudreaux, thank you for teaching me how to use my Magic List and for always putting a smile on my face.

To my beta readers—Amanda Holmes, Britt Bolnick, Juju Hook, Damian Boudreaux, and Michelle Stampe—thank you for your thoughtful feedback and great ideas!

To all the mentors and clients who have taught me so much over the years—especially Kyle Cease, Sean D'Souza, Russell Brunson, and Elizabeth Purvis—thank you. You have no idea how much your expertise and caring contributed to this content.

ABOUT THE AUTHOR

Julie Anne Eason helps people write and publish world-changing books that Inspire, Educate, and Sell.

She is an author, speaker, and CEO of Thanet House Publishing—a boutique book production company that helps people through the entire process from book development through publishing and distribution. She has ghostwritten multimillion-dollar books for thought leaders and influencers in a wide variety of industries. She also teaches writing and publishing through online courses, workshops, and events.

The struggles and challenges she overcame throughout her 30-year freelance writing career prompted her to write her own books, *The Profitable Business Author, The Work At Home Success Guide*, and most recently *The 5 Author Freakouts*.

Learn more at JulieAnneEason.com.

OTHER BOOKS BY JULIE ANNE EASON

Find them at JulieAnneEason.com/books

The gig economy isn't going away. In fact, it's only getting more crowded. It's time to work smarter, not harder.

With 30 years of freelance writing experience under her belt, Julie Anne Eason shares her strategies for finding clients, managing work-from-home stress, productivity, and overcoming the typical feast-or-famine roller coaster ride.

As a published author, you become the recognized expert in your field. Your book attracts customers, drives traffic to your website, and opens up speaking opportunities. But only if you get it written!

The Profitable Business Author is your step-by-step guide through the entire process of writing a book that matters—from first draft to publication and marketing.

THANKS FOR READING!

You've got stories to tell and books to publish. It's my sincere hope that this book gave you the tools and strategies you need to get your work out into the world faster (and as stress-free as possible).

As a writer, you know that personal recommendations and reviews are the lifeblood of an author's career. So if this book helped you, please consider writing a review, posting about it in your author groups, or sharing it with friends.

You can scan the QR code below to quickly jump to the review page on Amazon.

I can't wait to read your book!

Julie Anne Eason

Made in the USA
Las Vegas, NV
10 July 2022

51360335R00098